THE GRAIN OF WHEAT: APHORISMS

HANS URS VON BALTHASAR

THE GRAIN OF WHEAT:
APHORISMS

Translated by Erasmo Leiva-Merikakis

IGNATIUS PRESS   SAN FRANCISCO

Originally published under the title
Das Weizenkorn
by Johannes Verlag, Einsiedeln
© Johannes Verlag 1953

Cover by Riz Boncan Marsella

Unless the grain of wheat falls into the ground and dies, it remains alone.

Whoever wants to serve me must follow me.

—JOHN 12

CONTENTS

TRANSLATOR'S PREFACE

Hans Urs von Balthasar's style—always lucid, always precise—always partakes of the poetic as well. Indeed, an essential aspect of his quest for precision is elegance of form and depth of treatment. These, along with the intensity of his contemplative vision, have always been the hallmark of von Balthasar's writings. Since the author of these aphorisms saw fit to leave in the original texts borrowed from French writers, we have likewise decided to give the reader an occasional taste of Father von Balthasar's German.

The form of the aphorism, which he selected for the present volume, adds an intimacy of tone and a concentration of thought that make it unique among his books. As a kind of distillation of nearly everything von Balthasar pursues at length in the rest of his œuvre, this book's first quality is that it is highly practical for the reader on account of its brevity. As well, it presents a sharp challenge to both translator and reader (the translator being nothing but a particularly active reader) on account of its density of meaning and frequent ellipses—expressive leaps requiring vigorous collaboration with the author's thought at the levels of both language and life. These are texts, in other words, crying out for intimate, existential understanding and fulfillment.

The sovereign freedom of thought and the spiritual penetration these pages breathe should be an encouragement for readers of every tendency to move on beyond stale theological partisanship, to consider the fullness and dynamism of Christian truth in all its bright splendor.

To the merely conservative, for instance, von Balthasar says: "Everything human remains suspended; nothing human ought to become entrenched and hardened. Just think of the relationship between lovers . . ."; and: "Atheism can be like salt for religion. It is negative theology posited in the most absolute way. Most of the time, psychologically speaking, atheism represents a disappointment with the narrowness and limitations of a certain concept of God. . . ."

To the merely liberal: "The sense for rank and subordination is noble; the idea of individuals' equality of value and rights is bourgeois"; and: "Whoever wants to become green quickly remains on the lower branches. The noblest sap will not be seduced into the lateral boughs: it rises vertically and pushes the crown of the tree higher."

And to all of us alike, who so often suffer from a despair based on terminal self-reliance: "When we are exhausted—precisely in the midst of this exhaustion, this failure—we experience that it is he who has come to us. Exhaustion as the 'rustling sound' in which God is to be found (Elijah!)"; and: "A God who was a mason and a carpenter for thirty years can surely make short work of the ruins of my soul."

The fifty years since the first edition of *Das Weizenkorn* (1944) and the forty-one years since the second edition (1953) have done nothing to rob these pages of their relevance, bite, and ability to nourish even as they challenge. In the end, every careful reader of Hans Urs von Balthasar will discover that the precious alchemy of his thought results from the deeply fruitful marriage he achieves between keen intelligence and ardent piety. This achievement, doubtless the very heart of the Christian intellectual endeavor, in itself exposes the fallacy of one of the dominant dogmas of our time: the necessary dichotomy between "scientific" fact and "subjective" faith. We must note, however, that the religious path this Catholic treads has nothing to do with official pieties and spiritual programs but rather bespeaks intensely human experience: "The opposition of the 'dark tyrant' within us [to divine union] is so powerful that this self must slowly be broken up to the last grain, like a rock under the continual attack of the waves. It must crumble away, rot, burn up, until the way is finally open. And the greatest opposition comes from spiritual aspirations."

The reader will surely grow in the conviction that, if von Balthasar proves to be one of the scant few thoroughly reliable teachers and pathfinders in the thicket of late-twentieth-century life, it is only because he himself exemplifies the truth of his own aphorism that "only the one whose eyes can encompass much may be said to have an integrated vision."

Do not this great man's own life and work represent the Christian thinker's specific way of fulfilling the Lord's parable concerning the dying and rising of the grain of wheat? Aphorism by aphorism, book by book, trilogy by trilogy, he has squandered himself like nourishing bread.

E. L.-M.
Chihuahua, Mexico
28 June 1994
Feast of St. Irenaeus of Lyons

GOD

God's Face like a countenance beaming forth from the darkness: in order to see it we throw everything we possess into the fire—the world, our joys, our hopes. The flame leaps forth, consumes it all, and in its glow the beloved Face lights up. But the flame dies down, and we feed it with what little remains to us: honor, success, our will, the intellect, our temperament, finally our very self: *absume et suscipe*—"take and receive". This is not simple self-giving but, increasingly, the knowledge that I am being taken, that I must surrender. Grace is everything: the moment of God's appearing; grace also every sacrifice the fire snatches from me.

We cease to perceive water that continually flows. We hear our innermost wellspring, which flows forth from God, only when we make a conscious effort. This is why the saying of the Pythagoreans that the wise man perceives the music of the spheres is a truly religious saying. We should always be hearing, as with bodily ears, the gurgling wellspring of our origin in God.

We belong more to God than to ourselves; thus, we are also more in him than in ourselves. Ours is only the way leading to the eternal image of us that he bears within himself. This way is like a carpet rolled out from him to us, a scroll *prodiens ex ore Altissimi*— "coming forth from the mouth of the Most High"— and we should, like children, learn how to copy it, how to trace the pre-scribed, pre-written characters that have been presented to us. The pre-scription, the law, is what Love has written out in advance, what Love pre-supposes and proposes to us that we might . . . become it.

"The Life was the Light of men." An infinitely mysterious word: the Life—not understanding or thought—is the spiritual Light. The Life of the Logos, the divine Life—the Holy Spirit, *lux beatissima, lumen cordium*—"the most blessed Light, the Light of hearts". This Light is the true Life of souls, unattainable by any "psychology".

❖

"The bodily eye does not suffice to consider even a few of God's works. It is not satisfied with the unique contemplation of even one thing. After looking at it intently for a long while it still cannot tear itself away. How much less, then, will the eye of the soul suffice, even when it is lucid and awake, to consider the wonders and judgments of God."   BASIL

You will plunge most deeply into the foundation of existence if you consider *delight* to be the essence of your being. Hegel's infinite superiority to Schopenhauer. Absolute being is absolute delight, and therefore trinitarian.

"Was it not your bliss that you could never love as much as you have been loved?"   KIERKEGAARD

Holiness consists in enduring God's glance. It may appear mere passivity to withstand the look of an eye; but everyone knows how much exertion is required when this occurs in an essential encounter. Our glances mostly brush by each other indirectly, or they turn quickly away, or they give themselves not personally but only socially. So too do we constantly flee from God into a distance that is theoretical, rhetorical, sentimental, aesthetic, or, most frequently, pious. Or we flee from him to external works. And yet, the best thing would be to surrender one's naked heart to the fire of this all-penetrating glance. The heart would then itself have to catch fire, if it were not always artificially dispersing the rays that come to it as through a magnifying glass. Such enduring would be the opposite of a Stoic's hardening his face: it would be yielding, declaring oneself beaten, capitulating, entrusting oneself, casting oneself into him. It would be childlike loving, since for children the glance of the father is not painful: with wide-open eyes they look into his. Little Thérèse—great little Thérèse—could do it. Augustine's magnificent formula on the essence of eternity: *videntem videre*—"to look at him who is looking at you".

God gives us everything in order that we may give everything back to him. Thus, our all is his all—and we have nothing. He desires to empty himself in order that we might receive something. Now we have something, precisely our nothingness, and it is this that he is seeking. And yet we are robbed even of our nothingness, and we no longer have a right to consider it non-divine. Both things are now true: that we can truly choose to give him something, and that we cannot possibly hold anything back from him.

Time is the revealer of love through its manifoldness, through its slow unfurling of millions of possibilities. Time is the fully unfolded intensity of love, since within Time love can take on the wonderful meaning of a story, of a process. Even in a purely formal sense—quite apart from whatever happens within it—Time is God's most glorious invention, as revelation of his patience (because there is always more Time) and of his impatience (because Time is irreversible).

These little coincidences, these little attentions paid us by destiny, which make the impersonal tangible: an immediate transparency of a tender love that appears to be all the nearer as its pretext to flood us suddenly is all the slimmer. We must strive to become aware of such seconds.

All great persons are openly soaring questions on the horizon of the human race. All small persons shut in what is great, and from it they carve out for themselves a system and an idolatrous image.

L'amour est quelque chose de tellement beau, de tellement doux et qui me dépasse tellement, que je m'y abandonne sans comprendre. Et c'est une béatitude de plus de ne pas comprendre, car on sent que la source est inépuisable et qu'on peut s'enivrer indéfiniment sans la tarir; on sent que l'abîme est insondable et qu'on peut s'y perdre éternellement sans en toucher le fond: "Love is something so beautiful, so sweet, and which so surpasses me that I abandon myself to it without understanding it. And not to understand is but an added bliss, because you feel that the source is inexhaustible and that it can intoxicate you indefinitely without ever drying up. You sense that the abyss is unfathomable and that you can lose yourself in it eternally without ever touching bottom."   CONSUMMATA

"If it were a prerogative of love for it to love the extraordinary, then God would, so to speak, be in a tight spot, since for him there is nothing extraordinary."   KIERKEGAARD

God cannot have redeemed me merely because he

has also redeemed all others, because my relationship to him is never accidental. Therefore, without falsifying the truth, I am entitled to disregard the quantitative totally—with infinite gravity when I am considering Christ's suffering and Cross and with infinite joy when I am considering his personal, redeeming love.

God works the good even when he foresees the scandal it will cause. What a situation in Mark 3! Jesus sees himself over against those who cannot wait to take scandal at his goodness. "They kept silent. He looked angrily around him and, with deep sorrow over the hardness of their hearts, he said to the man: 'Stretch out your hand!' " How often does God have to work the good in anger and sorrow?

Perfect (intuitive) self-awareness would be an awareness of one's own origin from God and thus an indirect intuition of God. Perfect love of self would be a love of this origin from God, of this gift-quality of one's own being; perfect self-love would thus be indirect love of God. The deeper, therefore, one's love of self, the closer it is to the love of God, which does not abolish the former. This is said ontologically speaking, without prejudice to a practical education in the love of God, which naturally cannot be attained through introversion but only through the "leap out of oneself".

❖

"When we experience real [interior] thirst, it is the same as when we are thirsty because of the heat: we may do something other than drink, but whatever we do and whatever the company we keep— regardless of other desires, thoughts, or activities— the image of a drink never disappears from our mind as long as the thirst continues. Or take the case of someone who loves a thing passionately, with all his strength, so that nothing else gladdens him or touches his heart but this one thing and this thing only. Wherever the person is, in whatever company, whatever he may undertake or be doing: all that is loved in this way always fades away and in all things he finds an image of the one loved object. He who loves God does not seek for repose, because there is no restlessness in his life leading him astray. Such a person is all the more graced by God, as he values all things in a divine manner, indeed, higher than these things are worth in themselves. To be sure, zeal is required here, and the person cannot learn such a thing by fleeing; rather, he must acquire an interior solitariness regardless of where or in whose company he may be."   MEISTER ECKHART

❖

God is the only friend who does not abolish essential solitude. He is the friend, rather, in whom solitude as such becomes fulfilled. Not only because he is so light and unobtrusive, nor because he is so great that it is impossible to comprehend him, but because our deepest yearning for solitude is not at all a yearning for ourselves but for that interior love and dialogue that lie beyond the mere encounter of an I and a Thou—in a region where oneness and twoness have been left far behind us. . . .

Only the person who contemplates the beauty of nature in God and is accustomed to regard it as his voice, his sphere, the mirror of his countenance, can, even in his mature years, experience nature as naïvely and ecstatically as in his eighteenth year, without a drop of melancholy.

"The cause of all things is perfect in imperfect things, since it is primally perfect; but it is imperfect in perfect things, since it is also supra-perfect and prematurely perfect. That cause is form-giving form in unformed things, since it is primal form; but it is formless in formed things because it is also above every form. It is the essence that spotlessly enters all essences, and yet, being supra-essential, it lies above every essence. It delimits all primal reasons and imposes order, but at the same time it is sublimely above every reason and every order. It is the measure of the existent and of time, and yet itself is supra-temporal and pre-temporal. It is fullness in the void, super-fullness in the full, inexpressible, ineffable."

Dionysius the Areopagite

"No one better understands true distinctions than the one who has attained to unity." TAULER

It can be arrogance not to accept God's rewards and promises for the afterlife, that is, not to want to integrate them into one's motives for acting. But it can equally be selfishness to want to serve God on account of this reward, to want to become rich "off him". We escape the dilemma if we consider that our reward is God, that God is Love, and that Love does not look to itself, much less to a reward.

To live with another within the compass of one heart: I must move to the side, must make myself small, so that the other has space and does not feel crowded.

God wants for himself, at the same time, everything and nothing. Everything, because he does not give his honor to anyone else; nothing, because he already has everything, and, lover that he is, he wants nothing for himself. This is why he demands that we seek him in all things and that nevertheless the whole tide of our thanksgiving to him be diverted through the world. Thus, the indissoluble unity of contemplation and action has its foundation in God himself.

If anyone—God, for instance—takes away your coat, give him your shirt as well. And if anyone—God, for

instance—asks you to go ten miles with him, go the twenty.

What Nietzsche calls the "perspectivism of the world and of truth" contains a deep truth, but he draws the wrong conclusions from his insight. Relativity (with respect to God) is not relativism. We must grant, however, that Christian philosophy has only seldom drawn the ultimate consequences from its tenet that the creature is a *relatio subsistens*.

Les mêmes œuvres qui sont toutes nôtres sont encore mieux toutes siennes, parce que comme il les produit en nous, nous les produisons réciproquement en lui: "The same works that are wholly ours are even more so wholly his, because, just as he produces them in us, we produce them reciprocally in him." FRANCIS DE SALES

God is so wide that, within his spaciousness, even the longing for unfulfillable longing can soar freely. Gregory of Nyssa understood this best and gave an advance answer to Rilke's convulsed nostalgic pathos.

God is above us: hence our impulse to lose ourselves and turn everything human in us to coal. Christ is in us: hence our certainty that, in the infinite, we recover all of our dear finitudes like a grace.

"Through the being that it derives from him, the soul sees that it finds its natural life in God and its

spiritual life through the love that it bears him. Therefore does it lament and bewail its lot: that so fragile a life as the one lived in the mortal body should nevertheless be strong enough to prevent the soul from enjoying the powerful, true, and precious life that both nature and love would have it find in God."   JOHN OF THE CROSS

"God is more really experienced in renouncing than in receiving. For, when one receives, the gift has it in itself to gladden and console the receiver. But, if one receives nothing, then one has nothing, finds nothing, and knows nothing over which to rejoice except God and God's will alone."   MEISTER ECKHART

Through prayer we should come to perceive and savor God within us (the *interne sentire et gustare* of Ignatius). And yet, in prayer, we should not be seeking any enjoyment but rather the pure service of God. In order for us to learn how to unite both things, God takes us into his school, which consists in a continual alternation of consolations and abandonments, until we have learned how one can even enjoy in a wholly selfless manner and how to experience enjoyment itself as service.

Which of the two has loved more deeply: Hegel, the great matchmaker, who personified the impatience for marrying off and uniting; or Kierkegaard, who embodied the zealous patience for keeping the parties

apart to the end, only to make us fall to our knees the more definitively?

"If I had the firm conviction that no good comes from myself but that everything comes from God, it would in no way be irksome to me for God to reveal his works in me. It is also not irksome to me to hear others praised; rather is it a great joy to me and a great consolation to see how God shows his magnificence in them." TERESA OF AVILA

L'adoration, c'est l'amour écrasé par la beauté, la force, la grandeur immense de l'objet aimé; il tombe dans une sorte de défaillance, dans un silence plein, profond. C'est aussi le dernier effort de l'âme qui surabonde et ne peut plus dire: "Adoration is love overwhelmed by the beauty, the power, the immense grandeur of the loved object. Love then falls into a kind of faint, into a full and profound silence. It is also the final effort of a soul that is overflowing and can no longer speak."

ELIZABETH OF THE TRINITY

Oh, the tirelessness of God's love! Day by day to come personally into my soul, visiting it in human form just as men visit one another, in order—if the soul permits it—to build up his temple there, stone by stone, and not from a distance but with his own hand, as it were.

"All creatures tell, in their own language, what God is

in them, and their voices together make up a wonderful song. It is a silent music because it communicates a soft and tranquil sensation, untroubled by human voices, and simultaneously affords the enjoyment of sounds and the peace of silence." JOHN OF THE CROSS

"Supposing that the good Lord did not see my good works. . . . That would not worry me. I love him so much that I would want to be for him an occasion of joy even if he did not know that I was the one responsible. Once he knows it and sees it, then he is obliged, so to speak, to reward me. And I would like to spare him this effort." THÉRÈSE OF LISIEUX

The more we come to know God, the more the difference between joy and suffering becomes tenuous: not only do both things become engulfed in the One Will of the Father, but love itself becomes painful, and this pain becomes an irreplaceable bliss.

Purgatory: perhaps the deepest but also the most blissful kind of suffering. The terrible torture of having to settle now all the things we have dreaded a whole life long. The doors we have frantically held shut are now torn open. But all the while this knowledge: now for the first time I *will* be able to do it—that ultimate thing in me, that total thing. Now I can feel my wings growing; now I am fully becoming myself . . . .

Perhaps there is such a thing as shame of one's creatureliness, of lying so vulnerably open before God's glance. This shame is removed from us by a particular grace of innocence.

"What does it mean to love God? To strain one's soul continually, beyond one's powers, toward the will of God, with the goal and desire of giving him honor." BASIL

To behold God is at the same time to cast one's eyes downward, because God's innermost recesses are too pure, too far removed, for human sight. But precisely this looking away is true contemplation and the highest bliss.

"This is perhaps that final flame, which will fill the whole world and consume it: the appearance of God's Word in every creature, when nothing but the spiritual Light will shine any more for both the good and the bad. This is the Light which already fills all things secretly, but then it will fill all things openly. This is, I think, the flame that says of itself: 'I am a consuming fire.' For he will consume all things when he shall be all in all and alone appear in all things."

JOHN SCOTUS ERIUGENA

"The Godhead, my dear Theotimus, is to us what the air is to the birds and the sea to the fish. One day

we will fly through this divine element and swim in this sea and rejoice that our powers are not sufficient to embrace the whole space. It will be an ever-new delight for us to see that God—even if giving himself to us without restraint or limitation—still remains an abyss we are not capable of plumbing: we cannot enjoy him in a manner that does justice to the infinity of his perfections, for these shall always transcend our power of comprehension. Incomprehensibility is the essential mark of the beauty we will behold in paradise. This beauty would not be infinite, it would not be God, if we could comprehend it." FRANCIS DE SALES

MAN

Man was not created to become resigned but to die to himself and, having become Christ's possession, to possess all things with him.

The stronger a personality, the more real its communion with the whole of mankind. In such a person there takes form what in the mass is lived only in a muffled way. And the person, for his part, shares with the whole his own unique form and fullness. Individuals nourish one another not only by their reciprocal knowing and willing but also through the unity of their blood or, more deeply, of their being.

Meaning [*Bedeutung*] is always richer than interpretation [*Deutung*].

The Fathers like to stress the fact that man sums up and sets free all of nature's beings in himself. In this ontological universalism there are to be found almost more possibilities to understand in a Christian sense the cosmic "global feeling" of our time than in the epistemological universalism of the Scholastics (the soul as *quodammodo omnia* and as the *materia prima* of the spiritual world)—although both aspects are complementary. By virtue of my vegetative nature I can participate in the being of all plants: I know what lies in their being. Thus also for animal life. If we reflect on this, we will fully come to understand Paul's doctrine concerning nature's sighing and rejoicing along with us.

In creating man, the Creator seems to have intended to show how many variations can be invented from a single theme. It is also amazing how much music can be made with the few notes contained in five or six octaves, how many sentences and languages can be written with twenty-four letters. Always the same clear limitedness of the elements, together with the unforeseeableness of their combinations (*a priori* and *a posteriori*, idea and experience).

Most men are weaker repetitions, duller copies, of their unique originals. We may say with Heraclitus: "To me one man is worth thirty thousand", but we must not continue with him: "And the multitude is worth nothing", for the foundations and walls of the heavenly Jerusalem, too, require many stones, and only a few can be the pinnacles. The greater part of a violin consists of empty space, and the smallest part are the four strings, but the emptiness is indispensable for the fullness of the sound.

The darkness of matter is like the depths of the ocean, which we traverse like shimmering fish—the last, almost lost images of the sun.

Truth is not flat like a sheet of paper. It has a body, a third dimension. It has gradations, is hierarchical. What is true at one level is not necessarily true at another. For the person who has scaled the whole of truth it is possible to describe the positions of these levels and their relation to one another. The higher a level lies, the more a knowledge of it presupposes the moral preparation of the soul. This structure of truth makes blockheads think that truth is subjective. All truth is in fact objective, but not for everyone.

Dead nature (the mineral realm) attains to its qualitative variegation and depth only in the life of the vegetable and animal realms, and this life attains to its objectivity only in the spiritual realm. Here we have the basis for the possibility of nature's being redeemed along with man.

Conversio ad phantasma! Turning toward the "phantasm"—the empty and transitory appearance of things—as prerequisite and locus for all our certain knowledge! We see existent being in what is nothing, *as* being existing in nothingness: "Helios in a toad puddle." And even ourselves we finally behold only in this void: the at-home-within-oneself in the not-at-home-within-oneself. In each realm an abyss (of awe) separates the highest accomplishments from the class immediately below. Of the best there are only very few, and this is why these have the grace of being inexhaustible: Plato, Goethe, Mozart, Rembrandt, Bach. For their sake it is easy for us to renounce legions of respectable and decent accomplishments, since these are but intensified versions of our own possibilities. But the truly great ones appear as revelations of the inconceivable.

All things can be considered in two ways: as fact and as mystery. Simple people, farmers, for instance, can often integrate both ways in a lovely harmony. In children it would for the most part be easy to develop a sense for mystery; but teachers and parents can seldom generate enough humility to speak of it.

Only the person with a sense of symbolism has access to the world of the Gospel, because it always teaches in a concrete way. Our understanding of the Bible stops precisely at the point where we make of it a textbook of religion and morality.

Every philosophy we can encounter ends in idealism. Only revelation opens philosophy's eyes for a higher realism.

"A false alternative is offered us in the following distinction: whether I come to the soul of another through the object or whether the object only catches my interest through the soul of the other because that object occupies him. In the latter case a progressive impoverishment would set in, since the objects would be merely incidental. In the former case, by contrast, the soul of the other would be degraded to an impersonal subject for which objects have validity. Since soul and object, self-being and world, are correlatives, it is a misunderstanding to suppose that life could be reduced to a mutual understanding between souls, just as it is a misunderstanding to suppose that life consists in the mutual recognition of accomplishments and results."   JASPERS

Construire une théorie avec les pièces de mon ignorance: "To build a theory with the fragments of my ignorance."   STENDHAL

Problems do not exist in order to be solved; we can never get "behind" Being. We always look with mild contempt on everything we have solved. Problems should always become more luminous in the light of the great mystery in which we live, move, and have our being. A sense of mystery is a Catholic sense.

Nothing is so much the stigma of a mediocre spirit as the drive and the enthusiasm for the systematization of ultimate things. We want to have done with things, and in just this way we betray the fact that we

cannot have done with things. None of the great thinkers was a systematician. Plato was a seer and a dialectician. Aristotle was an empiricist and an aporeticist. Augustine was a lover for whom existence appeared bearable only in the open—in the lament of the night and of love. Thomas was a traveling researcher who blazed roads in the virgin forest of Being, without believing that he had thereby taken its measures (a "summa" is not a "system"). Hegel was a Dionysian enthusiast (when he becomes systematic he turns into a professor and falls prey to Kierkegaard's mockery). Goethe is magnificent in his balance between form and fullness: in the worldly realm, he possesses something like the power of binding and loosing.

"Every world that I recognize as different from my own indeed makes me aware of the particularity of my own existence: I am only one world, not *the* world. But, by the same token, that recognition raises me all the more decisively as a knower into that One Common World, for which all particular worlds, including mine, are but individual possibilities and realities. The circle remains."   JASPERS

Our thinking and loving should penetrate like X-rays through the flesh of things and expose the divine skeleton within them. This is why every thinker must be a religious person.

❖

The Fathers saw the whole of nature as a symbolism of the spirit. In nature, as in a mirror, the spirit comes to know itself. Thus, for Origen, animals are the sensory portrayal of human characteristics and vices. In this the Lord's parables prepared the way authoritatively. When in the parable of the maturing seed we read that it grows night by night and day by day, what else do day and night mean here but the alternating "weather" of God's graces, consolations, and trials? But it would really be too cheap a move to belittle the obvious analogies present here between Christian and Neoplatonic thought by stating that there is a "dependency" of the former on the latter: for what in the latter is spiritualistic allegorism derives in the former from a trinitarian structure of thought—the vision of the world in the Logos as Image of the Father. In direct contrast, the last few centuries have insisted on looking at the spirit and at God from the worm's-eye view of matter and naked "factualness". (A sign of this is all the nonsense that even the most skilled patristics scholars have produced on the subject of the symbolism of the Fathers.)

Two contrary propositions, held at a distance from one another, can both be true. But if they are brought close together, they lose their incantatory power and effect a mutual paralysis.

23

The marvel of the five senses: that we can possess the same world differently five times over, each time with a totally irreducible quality . . . what richness! And that we can then bring this richness together into a unity in our spirit, without dispersing the manifoldness of the qualities . . . what a gift! The uniqueness of the quality of each sense becomes clear when we consider that it becomes incomparable precisely in its perfection. Moderately good painting can be compared with average music. But for Mozart there exists no analogy in any other art, as also for Michelangelo and Donatello.

In this Schelling is right: artfulness is a part of the credibility of a philosophy. An artless thinker can produce little truth.

❖

At twenty you swore to yourself you would never write aphorisms. You hated them so thoroughly because, in the realm of knowledge, nothing appeared clearer than this law: that each individual truth attains its definite contours and appropriate depth only through its relation to all other truths—through proportion, weight, and distance. I did not understand this in the sense of a system, something that, already in my youth, was as irksome to me as too tight-fitting a sport shirt. But it did seem to me that there were propositions that acquired their true resonance only at a certain elevation above sea level, and some

24

only on the highest mountains: it was precisely this that needed to be made known. To proclaim them on the flatlands of the spirit meant robbing them of their mysterious splendor and, therefore, of their innermost essence.

But then it became ever clearer to me that, at base, passion had as its object the esoteric character of truth, and that no misuse could rob truth of that attribute. Truth is objective, to be sure; this does not mean, however, that it is accessible to everyone at every moment. It reveals itself to the worthy and, even then, only according to the measure of its own discretion. Rank and nobility so constitute truth's essence that they shine from its smallest particle. Truth protects itself against desecration. In the end, what vouches for even the fragmentary insights and opinions of a person is the coherence of his life and the passion with which it is lived. Just as sound makes music, so too does the modulation a person has vouch for his truth. Philistines have attempted to solve the problem of the secret fracture between "existence" and "being" once and for all by appealing to the abysmal puzzle of creatureliness—as if what confronted them were a mathematical competition for a prize. But an ellipse can never be a circle. In the face of such "solutions" we can really say: too bad for the nice problem!

There are two kinds of aphorisms. The first answers the need for intellectual synthesis. The second, the need for an infinite perspective on things.

It suffices to reverse certain dicta in order to make them true. For instance, *Alterius non sit qui suus esse potest*: "No one should belong to another who can belong to himself." Or, *Nemo contra Deum nisi Deus ipse*: "No one is against God except God himself."

It is remarkable how little a wise man is concerned with harmonizing philosophical systems.

For the person who loves, even the most esoteric problems of metaphysics always remain practical and relevant: for instance, the question of individuation, of the analogy of being, of the relationship between universal and particular. These questions accompany all his doing and thinking. He solves them through his life and, at the same time, poses them ever anew.

Women are more generous with their insights than men. For the former, life is work enough; the latter save up their truth for an isolated deed.

By virtue of the talent entrusted to him, which gives him the *ability* to say simple things, the true writer also possesses a grace which puts him *in a position* to say them, while the vast majority of people must keep them within themselves, unexpressed. Thus it is that the singer sings, while the many others who "can also sing" listen to him in silence.

A book is always a dialogue that could not take place.

The sexual drive is in the first place—in its broad understructure—a force of nature. But it also reaches through all spheres of life and of the spirit to reach the pinnacle of the heavenly mystery of Christ and the Church (Ephesians 5). The order and disorder of a person's sexual conduct are therefore to be assessed and considered according to that person's rank and power. But the Church cannot judge these things other than in a Christian manner, which means from the perspective of the highest sphere and source of meaning. Now this sphere is not completely shut to any person.

Shame is the center of man in perhaps a deeper sense than that referring to the proportions of the body. The ability to experience shame shows more drastically than usual that in nature everything negative also has a positive aspect. Sex is the decisive point of intersection between spirit and matter (person and individual). Here man conceals both the hybrid, almost grotesque character of his constitution (the locus of the comic, the utilitarian dimension of his purpose-free love) and also the deepest mystery of his likeness to God, the mysterious character of his personality. Shame is the wholly spiritual phenomenon pointing to this second aspect of man.

Against the usual opinion, we affirm that in youth a person is more reflective than in maturity. A young person is always watching himself live—"over the shoulder", so to speak. This results from the vanity and insecurity of youth, but also from its desire to grasp the moment totally.

The cult of youth is always a sign of the greying of a culture. Just as it is true that every stage of life has its own meaning, which resists functionalization, it is equally true that youth is internally disposed toward maturity and formation. To praise the condition of being young as an absolute, self-contained value, or even as the highest value, gives evidence of a disjointed hierarchy of values. Further proof is given by the kind of men, produced by youth movements, who remain permanently infantile. To be a child and remain a child before God is something totally different, which indeed requires human maturity.

"Evil is opposed, not only to the good, but also to itself."   BASIL

Catastrophic times are not suitable for developing a philosophy of history. We should beware of constructing necessities out of facts: for instance, from the absence of Christian art at a given moment in time to conclude that Christian art is an intrinsic impossibility or at least highly questionable, and so forth.

There is no doubt that the Catholic principle finds a natural basis in those societies that have a sense of rank and class. But this is not stated with regard to redemption as such, since here no man possesses a higher rank than any other. The statement applies to the natural establishment of the Church in the world and, at a deeper level, to the social structure of the Mystical Body of Christ.

Nothing gives me so much pleasure as my ability to extricate from the chaos of history the four or five figures who together represent for me the constellation of my own ideas and mission.

In the natural realm a healthy forgetting is the condition for further effectiveness. In the realm of grace this forgetting finds its truth and fulfillment in absolution.

❖

The melancholy pleasure we derive from giving ourselves to what is of equal or less worth than ourselves is nothing other than the dark knowledge that we are lavishly squandering ourselves. In loving God we miss that freedom and sovereignty we experience when we give ourselves away in loving books, flowers, clouds, people, because God's love always seizes us as beings beholden to it, even when we are truly making a gift of ourselves. What frees us in it is the infinite superiority of him whom we are allowed to love.

❖

At times, when we stand before works of art or also before people, we often feel the need to exert ourselves in bringing to life the dead, cold, alien existence before us and, as it were, making it talk. At such moments we can experience, as by a stroke of lightning, the great extent to which we actualize ourselves in all our love of creatures: we lend ourselves to things in order to receive ourselves back from them. It is as if a small, hard, cold object were thrown into our soul, and our soul warmed it and softened it and made it grow bigger, until what came out of it again consisted of our own substance as chief ingredient. Thus it is when we read a poem. And even when the seed planted in us is alive and has an activity of its own (as in the case of people or of the Word of God), the result remains thoroughly synergistic.

❖

The stimulating thing about Christianity—quite apart from its interior mystery, and in a purely exterior sense—lies in the fact that it can never be brought into a univocal relationship to the world. God would then be incorporated into our circles and could be dealt with as a particular figure within a field of action. This truth brings about the silent or open despair of all who are bent on power and on exercising a general's command of the field of battle. (We have only to think of the relationship between Church and State!) But the same truth likewise results in the grateful delight and mirthful smile of those who desire God's victory in all things.

The question whether there exists a natural disposition for the religious (that is, for sanctity) should be unanswerable. Surely all saints also possessed natural generosity, daring, persistence; but the question is only whether God had already put this disposition in them independently of their special vocation to sanctity, or whether this vocation was the reason for the developing of the disposition, or, finally, whether special gifts of nature were given to them with a view to their vocation. Here, as always, the relationship between nature and grace cannot be seen through.

It is very easy to ask Christians perplexing questions, because from the outside Christ's mysteries appear to be mere paradoxes, and it is very difficult to solve them at this level. (The attempt often leads to a false apologetics.) The chief concern here, rather, should be to awaken in the questioner an elementary sense for mystery and awe. Because most people have once been in love, they can be reminded of certain laws and experiences related to the love between human beings, and from here one can ascend to the love of God.

We will best grasp the unity of nature and grace, fear and love, if we consider the following: on the one hand, even the creature's distance from God ("nature")

as such belongs to the image of the Trinity in man, because it is possible only in the Son's distance of love from the Father; and, on the other hand, it is on this account that the Son can, and wants to, reveal to us God's interior life precisely in the emphatic form of creaturely distance, as "Yahweh's servant".

To be a person, a *causa secunda* [or "second cause"], is a kind of countereffect to creatureliness, that is, to the pure, "accidental" incidence of Being. The latter exerts such force and brings such pressure to bear that it produces something like a countermovement, as when a strong grade in the landscape makes the water from a fountain leap upward, or when the pressure from the earth's layers results in towering mountains. The greater and more impetuous the gift of Being from the side of God, the higher the torrent swells up as it returns to him.

Je ne crois pas que les hommes soient dignes de blâme de se confondre à la nature qui, par les mouvements du ciel, de l'air, des eaux, des choses inférieures, des quatre saisons de l'année, fait que le monde est dans une continuelle diversité, afin que, passant par cette multitude sans bornes, il ait un plus grand rapport à l'infinité de son principe: "I do not think men deserve blame for becoming lost in nature, which, by the movements of the heavens, of the air, of the waters, of all lower things, and of the year's four seasons, results in a world fraught with ceaseless diversity. Traversing this boundless multitude of variations, the world acquires a more intense relationship with the infinity of its principle." YVES DE PARIS

❖

Integration: Matter assumed into the spiritualized human body. It must consequently abandon its autonomy and hence its most sublime manifestations: storm, fire, sea. . . . Once in a human body, matter becomes wholly "invisible". And yet, its beauty is here unsurpassable, by the grace of the descending form. It was God's boldest plan to predestine individual spirits as matter for the highest kind of molding. Here too, by becoming a member of the Mystical Body, the spirit in a true sense gives up its highest natural manifestations: it must in some sense decline in order to enter into unity. But at the same time, through grace, it gains an unsuspected supernatural beauty.

❖

The Enlightenment is always wrong, because its ultimate goal is *to expose*. Grace, by contrast, is founded on truth, because it covers a multitude of sins. What God once and for all does not wish to know should never become the object of human knowledge and investigation.

❖

Du ciel même nous regarderons cette terre, puisque le fils de Dieu l'a regardée du ciel et l'a choisie pour sa demeure. C'est honorer Jésus d'honorer cette terre: "From heaven itself we will look down on this earth, because the Son of God looked down on it from heaven and chose it as his dwelling. To honor this earth is to honor Jesus."

BÉRULLE

✛

Our existence, in its very foundations, is structured for sacrifice. As we grow up we want to become something, to grasp, to climb; but then the curve takes a downward turn. Quietly life takes from our hands everything we have snatched up. In the end we are *granted the possibility* of dying and, with it, that of performing the highest act of homage before the Eternal One.

PARTING

All religions, except Christianity, want to offer man a support, a firm foothold within the eternal swirl of change, a refuge within the general ephemerality of things. For this were these religions invented: they are a flight from and a devaluation of temporality. But Christ accomplishes the opposite movement *into* time and, indeed, into its absolute futility. He does not sacrifice time; rather, he sacrifices himself within time. Whoever would enact his sacrifice along with Christ must renounce every support, every firm stance, every security and acquisition. This is why the Lord never compared himself with a saving anchor, a rock, or a house, but with the light, the spring of water, the life, the way; with a stone only insofar as it crushes or binds together in love as cornerstone; finally, with the door through which one *enters*, and with the resurrection that results only from the dying of the seed.

"God's commandments are to be fulfilled with an in-exhaustible yearning that is ever making haste."

BASIL

35

Every possible thought of moral progress I might entertain is dashed against the fact that I have not corresponded, with anything vaguely approaching due proportion, with the grace Christ has lavished upon me. I know myself to be ever more deeply guilty (and indeed not in the sense of some formula of humility, but in the face of very sober evidence) and yet ever more deeply graced. For these reasons, any self-assessment on my part becomes a definite impossibility.

We are always like people who have been carried away in their sleep over a deadly abyss. That we already *were* lost and, indeed, lost beyond all salvation, and that our present state of *not* being lost is nothing but the "accident" of grace: Who could get to the bottom of this thought?

The holy audacity and courage required in our dealings with God are not necessary because something must be "attained". On the contrary, they are necessary so that the soul will not give up in defeat as it recognizes the unattainability of perfection but will rather maintain the courage to continue walking with a firm heart its impossible path—the path upon which God becomes ever greater and man ever smaller.

It may be that in his expression Novalis remains too ambiguous and that his picture of the world means the dissolution of all stable form. What is stronger in him is his soaring sense of victory: he lives at the turning point that is Christ, in whom the old world becomes transformed into a new world through an absolute miracle.

"The person who reaches out for what lies ahead of him is always becoming younger than himself." BASIL

First of all, the ascent: nothing is pure enough for us; we can no longer bear what is ambiguous and facile (Wagner, then Beethoven). In order to be able to breathe we need the crystalline atmosphere, without the miasmas of earth (*The Art of the Fugue*). For a second we soar through the highest sphere into the empyrean (Mozart). There we encounter the divine child, Wisdom, who takes us by the hand and leads us back down the ladder. In the end she makes us hear the echo of her eternal melody even in the cacophony of our disc-players and tape-decks.

Progress toward God: as our soul is being purified, we become ever more aware of how much God's claims are increasing (in geometric progression, while I myself can in the best of cases advance only arithmetically). As more is accomplished, more remains to be done, so that a goal cannot be sighted. "Inadequacy here becomes event"—inadequacy in the double sense of God's incomprehensibility and of our own insufficiency.

Almost everything in the usual guidelines for spiritual progress is based on the unspoken principle: I must grow. When religion is not founded on security anxiety, the impulse toward "higher culture", "spiritual refinement", and so on, often plays the decisive role. We can live our whole life without ever realizing the meaning of: I must decrease. Not decrease exteriorly and grow interiorly; not decrease through mortification in order to increase in virtue according to the spiritual man; not decrease in "appearances" in order to grow in "essence"; but quite simply: he must grow, I must decrease.

Nicht Verachtung läßt uns über Geringes achtlos hinweggehn, sondern die Achtung vor dem Anspruch des Höheren. Das Schönste am Christentum ist es aber, daß der steilsten Sehnsucht der Prüfstein beigesellt wird: im Geringen das Hohe zu finden: It is not disdain that enables us to pass beyond the inferior without paying it heed but reverence before the claims of the superior. The most beautiful thing about Christianity, however, is that the steepest yearning must pass the test of finding the superior within the inferior.

❖

The never-returning moment when we, at age sixteen, see our whole childhood alive within us for the last time, and when we at the same time have a presentiment of our whole future life. . . . We know that tomorrow the door of the past will be shut, and we must now walk, mile by mile, the road we have surveyed from above.

Why is standing still already a going back? For the simple reason that all perfection consists in the very act of walking, in the *movement toward*. In Philippians 3:12ff., Paul says it clearly enough. In the language of Gregory of Nyssa and Augustine: since the creature *is* extension, a "tending-from-and-toward", its "perfection" must consist in the realization of this very "tending". With only slight exaggeration Augustine affirms: "Our perfection consists in knowing that we are not perfect."

Pendant que nous demeurons dans le péché, il n'y a rien à espérer pour nous. Mais tandisqu'un pécheur sent son poids et que son péché lui devient en effet un fardeau insupportable, il n'y a rien de désespéré pour lui: "While we abide in sin we have nothing to hope for. And yet, although a sinner feels the weight of sin and his sin in fact becomes for him an unbearable burden, no despair exists for him."   FRANÇOIS DE CLUGNY

The highly questionable character of many vows made by the "saints": they used them as ultimate assurances when what they should have done was to cast themselves adrift like a will-less piece of wood on the high seas of unfathomable Love. The same may be said for many of their penitential practices: it is as if they were keeping count, notebook in hand.

To say nothing of their famous "long prayers". From his experience with his fellow Spaniards, Ignatius knew what he was saying when he spoke of the hardening of the soul through such prayers.

Je dois m'ouvrir du côté du ciel plutôt que de me fermer du côté de la terre: "I must open myself up on the side of heaven rather than shut myself off on the side of the earth."   CONSUMMATA

It requires more humility to recognize one's hopeless mediocrity than to proclaim oneself a great sinner.

The more mature a person becomes, the more the category of the interesting loses interest for him. It is not even that other things become more interesting for him than former ones. The whole notion now simply escapes him.

The soaring of youth resembles those fountains you sometimes see in shooting booths at a fair or in farmers' gardens: at the top of the jet of water, up and down, a small colorful ball is dancing. Until we are thirty or so, a natural impulse pushes us upward; its purpose is to teach us elevated existence. Later on, the supporting jet runs dry, and we must know how to remain on high on spiritual power alone.

Whoever wants to become green quickly remains on the lower branches. The noblest sap will not be

seduced into the lateral boughs: it rises vertically and pushes the crown of the tree higher.

"We experience more joy and satisfaction in creatures when we renounce them. This joy will never be tasted by the person whose heart is always seeking to secure their possession."   JOHN OF THE CROSS

Nur wer viel übersehen kann, hat Übersicht: Only the one whose eyes can encompass much may be said to have an integrated vision.

Thomas Aquinas says that truth resides primarily in the thinking spirit but goodness primarily in the thing strived for. It follows from this that ethical transcendence is much more radical than theoretical transcendence. When we are engaged in thought, we always remain "at home within us" even in our most extravagant speculations. When we are engaged in action, however, our whole self risks being lifted from its hinges. It is not sufficient to *know* what lies beyond our self; everything in us must, so to speak, be thrown out of our windows.

Je crois que la connaissance de soi est un bon agent de sanctification, mais que pour l'acquérir, se disséquer n'est pas le meilleur moyen, loin de là! Il me semble que c'est plutôt en contemplant notre idéal que nous prenons conscience de ce qui nous manque. Nous n'avons pas besoin de mesurer les fils qui nous attachent au néant, ni de les

*compter pour les briser, afin de nous élancer vers le tout:
c'est par la force de l'amour qui nous porte au Père que
nous les rompons sûrement*: "I believe that self-
knowledge is a good agent for sanctification, but the
best means of acquiring it is not 'self-dissection', far
from it! It seems to me, rather, that we come to realize what we lack by contemplating our ideal. We
do not need to measure or count the strings attaching
us to nothingness in order to sever them, only then
to plunge into plenitude. It is surely by the power of
the love that carries us toward the Father that we
break them." CONSUMMATA

"What do you seek?" The Lord does not immediately say: "Come and see!" That would be dictatorial
and would do violence to the seekers, even if it were
what they themselves wanted. Nor does he ask: "Do
you want to come to me?" That would make it too
easy for them, and he must leave open the possibility
that they are seeking something else. God's question
is a facilitating invitation, which, however, does not
prejudice the human answer.

"Follow me." "Lord, let me first bury my father!"
So, Jesus calls forth a son from the midst of his first
sorrow. No time to lose: now is when he is open,
ripe for his best possibility. Only the person who is
certain he can make another happy ought to do such
a thing.

"If you seek me with your whole heart. . . ." Yes, Lord, then we have already found you. And if we are seeking you with only half a heart, you must show yourself to us earlier, otherwise we will never find you.

Before you exert yourself, be aware that before God every exertion is but a game accepted in grace, a game that is not of itself important but that grace draws into the sphere of the important. Allow the tension of your efforts to be enfolded by the relaxed abandonment of a child's helpless faith.

Wenn unsere Saiten gut gespannt sind, spielt Gott schon von selbst auf unserer Seele. Und mehr als dies sollen wir gar nicht: zu Gott hin gespannt sein: When our strings are well tuned, God can spontaneously play on our soul. And we should aim at nothing more than this: to stretch out toward and be attuned to God.

The negativity of asceticism: you can help only in clearing out the room, and even then most objects have to be torn from you against your will. The new furnishings are supplied and paid for by God alone.

Hesitation, despair, despondency are instances of ig-noble and impolite behavior toward the goodness and forbearance of God.

43

*«Vollkommenheit»? Ist ein Geschöpf denn je «voll gekommen»? Da es doch immer «nur eben erst ankommt»? Oder kann Gott, der Unendliche, je für ein Wesen «voll gekommen» sein? Aber eben in dieser doppelten Unendlichkeit liegt das Geheimnis der Liebe, die jeweils neu alle Grenzen überbordet. Die Unvollendbarkeit des Geschöpfs als po*tentia obœdientialis *zu Gott ist eine unschließbare selige Liebeswunde, in ihrem Offenstehen liegt alle Gesundheit und «Vollendung» der endlichen Wesen*: "Perfection"? Can we ever say that a creature has "come full way"? Isn't a creature always "only just arriving"? Or can God, the Infinite One, ever be said to have "come full way" to a creature? But it is precisely in this double infiniteness that the mystery of love lies, which is always overflowing all boundaries. The imperfectibility of the creature, as *potentia oboedientialis* toward God, is an incurable and blessed wound of love. In its remaining open lies all the health and "perfection" of finite beings.

Just as the Old Masters did, we paint ourselves as observers in the margins of the pictures of our deeds and prayers. But we shouldn't even sign them except by the character of our work, and it would be even better if the artist could not be recognized on the basis of the picture.

Our attitude with regard to God's consolations should not be different from that of the Poverello of

44

Assisi: he rejoiced in them as selflessly as in the flowers and the birds.

"I am convinced that an imperfect person needs more courage to walk the way of perfection than suddenly to become a martyr, since the struggle for perfection is not brief." TERESA OF AVILA

True poverty and, even more so, true endurance of insults and humiliations have one indispensable condition: the ability to be alone.

Every solitary hour that is truly such contains a challenge. That is why there is so little real solitude. Although we pretend to long for it, we avoid it and start up a noise within ourselves.

Solitude: the great disappointment of many who wish to be virginal for God's sake. They seek silence, a consecrated space, but in silence they find themselves and forget that true solitude, Christ's solitude, is that of the person deprived of rights, the person abandoned defenselessly to all the importunities of men: here there is no protection, no "enclosure", but only floating, adrift on the high seas. Here many a pious person has become a philistine.

"The life of man reaches fulfillment through a succession of many deaths." BASIL

45

Atheism can be like salt for religion. It is negative theology posited in the most absolute way. Most of the time, psychologically speaking, atheism represents a disappointment with the narrowness and limitations of a certain concept of God, an impatience stretching into anonymity.

Waiting for maturity is silver, making a decision is gold.

God gives us many things only so that we will sacrifice them to him. He himself assumed a body only in order to sacrifice it on the Cross and nourish us with it.

Let us not be seduced by a book's apparent location above the flux of time. Before God a book is as ephemeral as a word in conversation.

The element of infinity in Christian striving should not be confused with the Kantian and Faustian drive into the unbounded. The latter rests on the conceit that nothing is sublime enough to satisfy the abyss of my thirsting self. In this view, consequently, the God who created the satisfaction of this infinite element in me could never be objective, but only the Self of my self. The Christian infinite, on the contrary, consists in the fact that the shell of my self is too shallow to contain the unsurpassably greater God, and my will too dull ever to satisfy his infinite will to love. It takes humility to admit to ourselves that God can satisfy us completely, indeed, that it isn't at all our own intimations and yearnings that give the full measure of the extent to which we can be fulfilled. The burning of the heart to which God speaks is an infinitely blissful unrest, the very opposite of the endless and fatal conflagration in the heart of Faust or Don Giovanni. The Christian, too, can suffer endlessly if he seeks to correspond fully with God's will for his Passion, if he wishes to exploit fully, for the salvation of souls, the possibility of atoning through suffering in this life, before the arrival of the great Sabbath. The Faust-minded, by contrast, suffer out of pride, because to them the admission that their wishes can be fulfilled appears to be a defeat.

It is strange to see how sharp the dividing line is between those people who are satisfied with an ordinary, quiet life and those who strive for the extraordinary. The latter are rare, and you can almost always discern them from a distance. There does indeed exist as well an unhappy intermediate group, consisting of those who are only just capable of envisioning a higher existence, but these know that they lack the substance to realize such an existence in their concrete lives.

How difficult for God the education of his chosen ones, particularly his priests! He must endow them richly, so that they will become storehouses for their communities. At the same time, he must make them poor as beggars, so that they will refer everything to him, even in the face of their most lively and personal effectiveness. They are to be rich only for others; they must possess without knowing it or heeding it; and they must also know what riches are without seeking them for themselves. Humility involves paradoxes that are much stranger than we normally think.

"We can desire, out of self-love, to be delivered of self-love, and out of arrogance we can long for humility. There exists an endless and imperceptible recycling of ever-new reflections of the self. In us there always remains a certain substratum, a certain root of egotism, which is unknown and unattainable for the whole of our lives. It is God's will that we men should live in this condition here on earth." NICOLE

It is always the same old story: from among the mass of people one person awakens. Like Saul, he rises head and shoulders above the crowd. He begins to acquire vision. He not only *feels* he has a call to proclaim this vision, he actually has it. But, in the measure that he grows and his soul is filled, he becomes incomprehensible to the mass, and no one listens to him anymore. In the end he dies buried under his own plenitude, and a monument is set up over him.

It can be pleasurable to be despised by the mass of people. Here, once again, humility and arrogance rub

shoulders. Many a Christian in the world, many a Catholic within Christianity, and many a person within the Church suffers ostracism for personal or professional reasons, and precisely such people must carefully examine their motivations.

After all is said and done, death still remains the decisive situation of life. From it everything Christian could be derived. Fénelon used to say that the art of asceticism consists in the soul's dying before the body. Paul's *mortui estis* ["you have died"] in the end includes not only continual mortification but also the knowledge that everything that has not yet died possesses a merely preliminary character (this includes my virtue and my whole spiritual life and effort). Death is above all poverty, but also obedience and chastity.

La mort, c'est comme d'être fixé à jamais au point culminant, c'est d'être arrivé et demeurer au maximum de Gloire et d'Amour qu'on puisse donner à Dieu: "Death is like being established forever at one's apex. It is having arrived at and abiding at the maximum quotient of Glory and Love one is capable of giving God."

CONSUMMATA

"The more the consolations I believed I was losing for the Lord's sake, the greater the joy occasioned in me by this loss." TERESA OF AVILA

49

❖

Lorsque tout semble nous sourire à l'extérieur, c'est alors que Dieu nous immole le plus, et il cache admirablement son glaive sous ce qui s'appelle des «joies»: "When everything seems to be smiling at us from the outside, it is then that God is immolating us most intensely, and he hides his sword admirably under what are called 'joys'." CONSUMMATA

❖

"A weak soul does not find its bliss by sharing that of a holy soul, and a holy soul does not find its bliss by sharing that of an angel. Rather, if the weak soul wishes to become blissful, let it strive toward what makes the holy soul blissful." AUGUSTINE

❖

The only reason we cannot establish a personal relationship with God is that we lack fidelity. We must persevere in the knowledge that all our deeds and thoughts always stand directly before God, in total nakedness. Therefore, the smallest thing we do is related to him. Whoever has the courage to be faithful necessarily embarks on a personal relationship with him.

❖

Nothing is more boring than a complicated soul, nothing more gripping than a simple one.

❖

A God who was a mason and a carpenter for thirty years can surely make short work of the ruins of my soul.

Many seek to attach themselves rigidly to God in order to grow together with him. But God must shake them off roughly like irksome ticks.

Above all, we must not wish to cling to our suffering. Suffering surely deepens us and enhances our person, but we must not desire to become a deeper self than God wills. To suffer no longer can be a beautiful, perhaps the ultimate, sacrifice.

Il me semble qu'en montant de soi-même, on est vite limité par ses propres forces, et que, si l'on arrive à la sainteté, ce n'est jamais qu'une sainteté personnelle et limitée. Tandisqu'en descendant dans sa misère, en s'anéantissant, il me semble qu'à la dernière limite du «moi» on tombe en lui, et que c'est là la vraie sainteté, la sienne: "It seems to me that, when we rise on our own, we are quickly limited by our own forces, and, if we arrive at sanctity in this way, it will always be a merely personal and limited sanctity. But if we go down into our wretchedness, if we become nothing, it seems to me that, when we reach the outer limit of our self, we fall into him, and that is where true sanctity is to be found: *his* sanctity."   CONSUMMATA

Wandlung: als Wanderung, Hinwandeln. Darin: Wandlung als Veränderung, in eine Fremde wandern, in ein Fremdes sich wandeln, sich selbst entfremdet. Darin: Wandlung als Verwandlung, als Transsubstantiation:

Change: in the sense of wandering—wandering toward. Therefore: change as mutation, metamorphosis, entering a foreign land, changing oneself into something unfamiliar, becoming estranged from oneself. Therefore: change as transformation, as transubstantiation.

"This dissatisfaction with oneself and this sorrow over the fact that the soul does not serve God, does not revere and prize God far above all of the works it has accomplished and all of the consolations it has received. . . ."   JOHN OF THE CROSS

CHRIST

As when the huge red curtain parts in the middle and the announcer appears by the footlights (invisible behind him the mystery of the stage, he himself in some sense the embodiment of the drama that is about to unfold): thus did the Lord appear in the world.

All great thought springs from the conflict between two dominant insights: that the rift in Being is incurable and that it must nonetheless be healed. Since the solution of this contradiction lies in the hand of Christ alone, all philosophy is oriented toward his existence. Philosophy looks up to Christ with the same worried expectation of a dog looking at his master: Will he make up his mind to throw him the bone that will busy him for the rest of the day?

Nowhere is the creaturely nature of our thought more emphatically evident than in the problem posed by the clash between "to be" and "ought to be". Here it is clearly shown to us that there are problems we are not intended to solve, no more than Adam should have eaten the apple in paradise. For, on the one hand, we are not permitted to think that everything already is as it should be: no one has the competence to calculate sin into a stable picture of the world and thus usurp for himself the vantage point of the redemption, which God alone occupies. But neither are we entitled to doubt the fact that everything is as it should be, that is, that God's will is absolutely superior to man's and that it does prevail against it. The sting of this *aporia* makes itself keenly felt in a practical way when we must unite an absolute impatience with regard to sin with an absolute calm that trusts in God—a dead-serious desire to have the world be different with an equally dead-serious desire that nothing should be other than God wills it. Once again, the problem must be relocated, transferred into Christ. For him it was unbearable that the world should be as it was, and so he bore the unbearable in obedience to the Father. The real Passion lies at the crossroads of these two things; but there we also encounter the overcoming of the contradiction in the one and only Cross.

Everything physical is also a moral reality. The Fathers describe the event of Christ's Incarnation in the womb of the Virgin as a marriage between the divine and the human nature, whose fruit is the Mediator with the two natures. This implies that the nuptial covenant between God and man was concluded, consciously and deliberately, in the spirit as well. The

54

angel's annunciation is God's wooing of his bride, and Mary's assent incorporates the whole of human nature. We may then say that God never did violence to us, overpowering us without consulting us. The cooperation of man is already brought into play in the act of revelation itself.

✠

Christ as recapitulation of creation: as new Adam he encompasses everything human, but he also incorporates the animal realm in himself, since he is lamb, scapegoat, sacrificial ox, ram, and lion of Judah. As bread and as vine he incorporates the vegetative. Finally, in the Passion, he became a mere thing and thus reached the very bottom of the world's structure. This reification is most evidenced in the sacraments and especially in Christ's quantification in Communion wafers and in his multilocation: Christ as printing matrix, as generic article. Such reification has its cause, not at all in a subsequent desacralization of the holy by the Church, but in an intensely personal decision of the Redeemer and in the strongest possible effects of the redemption itself, whereby the Lord makes himself irrevocably a thing at the disposal of anyone who requests it.

✠

In Christ is fulfilled the longing of every artist to enter into his work, there to exist not only as objective but also as subjective spirit. For in the case of Christ we must not only say, with Augustine, *factus est qui fecerat* ["he who had created was now himself created"] but *factus est quod fecerat* ["he was made to be *what* he had made"].

Christ's holy humanity as embracing all that is possible in this world, as plaything and universal instrument of love: abraded by rolling in every gutter and every possible hell, shattered in the abyss of all nights, cast up to the heights of bliss, fragmented as food in a billion places and yet located above space, no longer time-bound as we are and yet not outside of time but always sharing in our own temporal condition and history. . . . In Christ is found the experience of all situations, existentially: the sum total of the world's reality.

Christ's arithmetic never works out neatly. He is always at once too rich and too poor, supremely powerful and powerless, active and passive. He is after all God and Man, head and body, and as such he is the measure for all things, and he makes every other measure—thank God!—inconsistent and unreliable. This is a personal measure, for the unity in Christ of the God who gives grace and the Man who receives it, of heavenly and earthly truth, was produced, not through the identity of one nature, but in the identity of one Person. Regarding this subject, even whole continents are but a white dot on the maps of theology.

We could ask the question whether some sphere

does not exist in which the categories of act and potency no longer suffice for the description of the most real kind of Being. I mean the sphere of love. Here abundance is always neediness as well, and poverty wealth. The lover does not possess what he has not yet given away, and the beloved possesses everything that, not he, but the lover has. To say that God is "pure act" is in keeping with Hellenic thought. To do justice to Christian thought we would have to conceive of the triune tide of God's life as a reality beyond act and potency. And this pure and eternal flowing of the divine life is revealed by Christ in a created vessel.

It is difficult to make young people understand the real mystery of Christ, because the mystery of weakness runs counter to the impulses of youth.

We cannot look directly at Christ any more than we can look directly at the sun. He has to be "interpreted". His works, words, miracles are one and all signs that point to something: they do not signify only themselves. They possess an unbounded depth into which they attract and invite us. But we do not find the truth *behind* them, at a second, purely spiritual level (as the Fathers often thought: that was the eggshell of their Platonism). Rather (and the Fathers affirmed this as well): the Word became Flesh, the eternal Meaning has become incarnate within the temporal symbol. What is signified must be sought within the sign itself, the "moral" within the history, the God within the Man. No one shall ever leave Christ's humanity behind as obsolete instrument.

Il n'y a moment, il n'y a lieu, il n'y a circonstance qui ne soit illustrée ou de l'opération ou de la suspension de quelque grâce ou effet admirable que l'humanité de Jésus devait porter en elle: "There is no moment, there is no place, there is no circumstance that is not illumined either by the operation or by the suspension of some grace or admirable effect that the humanity of Jesus was intended to bear within itself." BÉRULLE

All external scenes of Jesus' life and sufferings are to be understood as a direct revelation of the interior life and intentions of God. This is the fundamental meaning of biblical symbolism and allegory, without which the whole gospel remains nothing but superficial moralism. Thus, for instance, Jesus' silence before Caiaphas, the *Ecce Homo* episode with Pilate, the figure of the Lord covered with the cloak and flogged, his nailing to the Cross, the piercing of his Heart, his words on the Cross, and so on. All of this is a direct portrayal and exegesis of God (John 1:18), accessible to the senses.

From this perspective it becomes obvious that the scenes with Mary and Peter must be understood in a Catholic sense, that is, "symbolically". This implies in no way a departure from the literal sense but, indeed, rather its fullness and fulfillment.

The continual interpenetration, in Christ, of the Lord and the Servant. How, as Servant, he reigns royally and how he serves humbly as Lord. And, for this very reason, there is nothing either domineering or servile about him. When he serves, he never lets you forget that he is the Lord (for instance, at the washing of the feet), or, when he rules, that he does so only as Servant. This gives us a direct insight into his divine Being, which, at the same time, is ultimate autonomy and ultimate dependence on the Father. And yet this is not a vision only of what is distinctive about the Person of the Son: in this vision we have a glimpse of what is common to the divine nature of all the Persons, since the Son reveals the Father in the Holy Spirit.

How do we know that God hates sin? By the fact that Christ loves sinners. These are the poorest of all, the ones most needing protection.

The parable of the barren fig tree as a wonderful earthly likeness of the intra-divine "consultation" between justice and mercy. The One appears here as divided into two figures, the Lord and the Gardener, but in the end the Gardener is really one with the Lord: "If not, you can have it cut down." Thus, too, the Son can be both one and not one with the Father.

❖

Are there, then, two different kinds of love, since

Christ loves the Father on account of his infinite plenitude and the poor, the abandoned, and sinners on account of their helpless emptiness and impotence? Is the second love only an "assignment" or task imposed by the first? Or shouldn't we say that even the second love is a reflection of the first, insofar as the world's poverty and impotence reflect something of the utter nakedness and self-abandonment of intra-divine love, and that therefore the Son seeks and finds the Father, and the Father the Son, in us?

In Christ, God and man reflect one another unto infinity. On the one hand, he is the result of the encounter of the two natures, but, on the other hand, as divine Person, he actually determines the very relationship and distance between God and man. As Redeemer he is "after" sin, but as Archetype and Head of creation he is "before" it. When on the Mount of Olives he drinks sin's distance from God and its judgment to the dregs, this is not only the passive portrayal of the distance between God and man; it is equally its active establishment in himself. But this also makes the sinner enter a strange, inextricable dialectic: he can no longer understand his temptation as anything other than a participation in the sufferings of the Lord, insofar as he is the Archetype. The sinner's abandonment by God has its measure and its meaning in the Lord's abandonment by God. And yet, at the same time, this thought must appear to the sinner an intolerable blasphemy, since at this moment every comparison of his own suffering with the Master's can only increase his suffering by adding to it an infinite element. Precisely this dialectic of being repelled by the grace of participation belongs to the essence of Christian suffering.

In the Lord's parables we may contemplate the problem of aesthetic form in its greatest purity: an infinite content becomes transmuted into symbols within a finite form, and this form opens up to the "inspired" hearer ever-new perspectives reaching into infinity. This occurs, moreover, without the form ever leaving behind its finiteness and becoming rarefied into spirit.

In all his actions, words, and so on, Christ, being God and Man, is always both Archetype and Image, Form and Mirror, Model and Imitation, Lord and Servant. Everything about him is a question and a call by God to man and at the same time an answer by man to God. It is an apologetical oversimplification when the Fathers divide the Lord's words into those he spoke as God and those he spoke as man. The sufferings of the Lord, for example, are at every second just as divine as they are human: they are a revelation of God to man and a self-surrender of man to God. Two paths are trod simultaneously in Christ, two opposite currents intersect in him: that from heaven to earth and that from earth to heaven. More precisely: Christ is *both* the unmediated unity of the divine and the human natures within the simplicity of his Person (and to that extent every one of his statements is a simple symbol that expresses this unity) *and* also the representation of the infinite distance between God and creature, exponentially raised and abysmally ruptured by sin (and to that extent his deeds and words are dialectical).

Christ portrays the love between God and man both from the side of its *polarity* (because every love demands two separate poles and suffers no amalgamation) and from the side of its *unity* (because in his Person simple love is evidenced beyond all tensions, and this is why his Person can only be divine). This enormous double signification that Christ represents is, in turn, possible only because it is a revelation of the Trinity: of the distance between Father and Son, in the unity of the Holy Spirit, as an autonomous Person. Christ's essence is itself trinitarian. Once this has been understood, then we can contemplate the whole gospel as the direct disclosure of trinitarian life.

Every moment of Jesus' life has an eternal meaning: it is taken up into his eternity and represents not only his abiding in his Mother's womb but also his dying on the Cross and his Resurrection. He is now, simultaneously, everything that he could then be only within temporal succession. This is why Mary, too, eternally remains in the situation of the Pregnant Woman—like the envelopment through which alone

Christ operates—and also in the situation of the Woman Giving Birth and of the Mediatrix of Graces. In this form of Christ's "omnitemporality", we can see something of our own form of existence in eternity.

"In his suffering Christ gave us to understand that the majesty of him who sent him is supra-infinite. Neither creatures nor life nor death could render him all the honor possible. And so he united the Creator with his work, the Infinite with the finite, Glory with disgrace, and he heaped all sins upon Innocence himself. His intention in so doing was that the master design resulting from the union of human and divine nature, of Being and non-being, of the All and the nothing should produce a kind of wonderfully invented homage, and that from the accumulated sheaf of such extreme opposites there should spring forth one single unrepeatable fullness of veneration and worship. The sacrifice of Jesus Christ is the ultimate effort of the divine Wisdom to fashion the work of art capable of rendering to the Infinite the totality of all possible homage." CONDREN

Humanly speaking, the Lord is astounding because he displays a purely divine quality—that of being at once wholly universal and wholly concrete—now within the human reality. Thus did he truly become all things to all men, and he simultaneously stands on every level of human experience and is to be found in every human situation, even in those that fully contradict and exclude one another. And yet, in so doing, he does not cease being wholly human. And he gives his holy ones a participation even in this quality. Now, if every Order has its own charism, participation in this quality of Christ's should be the charism of the Society of Jesus.

We often forget the bitter dregs at the bottom of the eucharistic chalice, the cup that is the memory of his suffering. "The chalice that is poured out *for* you", says the Lord, and he passes over in silence the fact that it is poured out *by* us. We receive him in the sign and condition of death, of ultimate self-surrender, which, as such, connotes the most extreme weakness. "We are the ones who immolate him," says Cyril of Alexandria, "for the immolators are those for whom he died, even if his physical death was caused by persons other than ourselves."

Only in Christ are all things in communion. He is the point of convergence of all hearts and beings and therefore the bridge and the shortest way from each to each.

Every manner of relation among men is a metaphor for the relationship to God and its inexhaustible wealth of ever-new perspectives. Christ calls himself our Master and our Friend. He calls us his brothers, sisters, and mothers. He is, therefore, the "child" of our soul: he is born in our soul of the Father but not without our cooperation. And yet he is also our mother, as we see in the image of the hen and her chicks. In a similar way, Paul's relations with the Christian community are so rich that he can describe himself as their father, wet-nurse, teacher, friend, and brother.

Amor and Psyche. A young woman falls in love with an unknown man and for years does not cease longing for him. One dark night he comes and unites himself to her. "May I look upon you?" "Our son will be the mirror in which you will see me." And what if this invisible nocturnal lover should be a god—should be God himself?

Among other reasons, Mary is the Mediatrix because it was through his Mother that the Lord learned what human love means. Through her he enters the living Tradition of all who pay reverence to God. In every respect, Mary has the role of concretizer: whoever rejects her must also reject the principle of the Tradition. Without her the Lord becomes an abstract principle of redemption.

Whoever has a taste for the divine and finds his joy in it will find in Mary the object of an analytical science that, from inferences drawn from just a few tenets, can attain an infinite, never-ending breadth of meaning. Three premises suffice: her identity as

Mother of God, her virginity, and the fact that, in the order of the Incarnation, no physical reality can be posited without its referring symbolically to spiritual realities. This last premise, which Augustine and all the Fathers insist upon, is evident in the case of Christ's Person even to Protestants of deeper vision. Symbolism thus understood is the decisively Catholic factor, and it prompts the kind of deduction that, as such, is not at all "mystical" or merely "edifying" but strictly objective and even scientific. Such, for example, is the derivation of Mary's role as Mediatrix of graces or her Immaculate Conception.

Whoever grants that motherhood is more than a purely physical event must look upon Mary's Immaculate Conception as a self-evident reality. How could the soul that participated in the formation of the God-Man be touched by the slightest stain? The great extent to which Mary's soul was indeed involved in this event is shown by her dialogue with the angel, in which the virginity of her soul is seen to be Mary's true womb. When, later on, Jesus goes about with sinners, or, better, when he eucharistically goes *into* sinners, he does this as the perfectly Pure One who purifies everything he touches. But the crux of the matter here is the manner itself in which this Pure One was formed.

The wedding of Cana. There is no room for the woman in the work of the man, which is now about to begin: election and mission, action and teaching. Her plea, which emanates from her feminine compassion, is inopportune: it disrupts the masculine plan. "Woman, are your concerns mine?" And yet, it is precisely as one rebuffed that she knows her plea will be granted: "Do whatever he commands you." And what was not the man's will becomes such through the woman's inopportune intervention. The battle between the sexes, too, belongs to the *forma peccati* [the "shape of sin"]: conquered by the second Eve, the second Adam accomplishes the deed of redemptive obedience and so reveals his glory before the world. According to Paul, the woman is the glory of the man.

All great heresies strike Christ on his most sensitive and painful spot: on the center of his love. They always argue away either the divinity of his humanity or the humanity of his divinity, under the pretext of an alleged purity.

The courage of Christ: to take his stance in the most vulnerable location possible, to place himself between sin and God's wrath—the very spot where the lightning bolt (and what lightning!) must strike him. But he lacks every trace not only of fear and insecurity but also of bravura. Rather, he is the very embodiment of simple, trusting shelteredness. What can happen to him? Fall out of the Father's hand he cannot, since he has himself chosen absolute dependency, or, rather, since from all eternity he *is* absolute dependency.

"Whoever follows me" follows a person, not an idea. The light of an idea is always available: "Your hour is always present." But when Christ speaks of himself as the Light, he does so with a kind of hurried urgency, as if he were a setting sun, as if he were entering his last quarter, as if night were already falling. Such is personhood.

"Why, O Lord, did you say: 'As long as it is still day'? Listen to the reason: 'The night is coming when no one can work.' Not even you, O Lord? Will that night have such power that even you will not be able to work in it, you whose work the night is?"

AUGUSTINE

❖

How carefully God must walk among men in Jesus! Each of his words is intensely circumspect, each of his steps is taken as if between two abysses of anger! So also in his education of the individual soul: we see one instance of this in the relationship between what is said and what remains unsaid. Just as we do not let children know anything of the celebration that has long been prepared, so too does the Lord work silently in souls. The adults are allowed to look behind the scenes of the Christmas preparations; but then they also have to help with them. Every fulfillment means an obligation.

God sees the greatest value in man's being present at Christ's sacrifice. He has so staged the great play of the Passion that the players have been brought together from the three great realms of mankind: Christians, Jews, and pagans. The great event of the drama is the world's decision against God. This decision begins in the innermost sanctuary of the Church, who, with a certain consistency, delivers her Lord to the people of the Old Covenant. Here the drama continues, since the Old Covenant pushes the Messiah off on the pagans and wants to recognize no lord but Caesar. From the divine perspective, all players are convicted by their own collaboration, and the more they try to disentangle themselves from responsibility in this divine action, the more surely they become enmeshed in it. All of us must give our approval to our redemption; even Mary had to do this when, at the foot of the Cross, she willingly accepted the blow from the sword in her Son's hand whereby he withdrew from her as Son (just as the Father had withdrawn from him). This event merely revealed the full depth of the assent she had once given the angel.

The real essence of Christ's Passion consisted in the two things we least like to bear and suffer: fear and disgrace.

❖

Like everything in his temporal existence, the Lord's sufferings were at the same time supra-temporal:

every moment of his suffering has an "eternal" intensity, and, precisely because of this, it towers far above chronological time. Thus we can in truth say that he suffers until the end of time. The fact that at the same time he can abide in a glory from which all suffering is absent is a contradiction only for our temporal manner of thought. The most contrary currents converge "at the same time" in Christ's supra-temporality as in an ocean.

Jesus before Herod: the eternally thought-provoking situation of God's persistent silence before a man who wants to force him to talk and would like to turn him into a religious sensation, an "experience", in Pascal's sense.

Jesus' sufferings, in the end, were suffered only for the Father; they were "open", so to speak, only in the Father's direction. Never will an individual man or the totality of all humanity even approximately grasp and encompass these sufferings. The visible Way of the Cross with its physical events is only a weak image and symbol of the abyss of Jesus' interior sufferings. Not everything about these is intended as a model for the world: a great part of them belongs only to the Father.

Why not expand our knowledge of Jesus and his interior life through the vast spaces of the Old Testament, amplifying it there as in a sound chamber?

Correctly understood, in the manner of the Fathers, the Old Testament is not only a prophecy but the very shadow of Christ. Thus, unless it is understood as a foreshadowing of Christ, the whole Book of Job remains an incomprehensible puzzle and even a scandal: for how could a man who declares himself to be just and wants in no way to acknowledge his guilt be justified by God before the whole world? Job's speeches could be interpolated between Jesus' seven words on the Cross: they are the Passion verbalized. The same holds for Jeremiah, all the other prophets, and the whole of the Law.

"Everyone who clings to Christ possesses—even if he does not understand them—all of the goods contained in the letter of the Law. Everyone who is foreign to Christ understands nothing and has nothing."

AUGUSTINE

The principle of the harmony between nature and grace is surely justified as a corrective to erroneous teachings. But not on that account should we overlook the enormity of the paradox that lies in the fact that this human life of ours—which is submerged in the bodily, the instinctual, and the terrestrial—has nevertheless been chosen as the bearer and expression of the divine Life. It is as if an oak tree were transplanted into a flower pot. The organic "elevation" of nature to "supernature" continually has its counterpart in a kind of ecstatic bursting open of nature.

The Lord's abandonment on the Cross is the emptying out of the sea of divinity: the chasms, shapeless and cruelly exposed, gape up at heaven. Love's negative side: an infinitely burning thirst, to be quelled by nothing but the very Love that has been eternally lost (John of the Cross, in his portrayal of the "dark caverns" in his *Living Flame of Love*).

The distance between the Lord, abandoned on the Cross, and his Father reveals not only sin's distance from God but also the infinite, incomprehensible, abysmal vastness within God himself, the expanse existing among the divine Persons. At the same time, however, an utterance such as "I and the Father are one" opens up a wide vista into their no less inconceivable nearness: into their identity of nature.

Der Doppelsinn des Wortes Umsonst trifft ins Schwarze des Christentums. Die Gnade ist vergeblich: sie vergibt: The double meaning of the word *Umsonst* [both "gratuitously" and "to no purpose"] hits the bull's-eye of Christianity dead-center. Grace gives away "for nothing": it for-gives.

Man is powerlessness, not-being-able. God's love is as much his adapting to our condition as his saving us from it. Because Jesus became powerlessness itself, it is now easier to be powerless (since such powerlessness bears the fragrance he exuded in his passing among us; or rather, the fragrance of his presence among us now). At present, impotence is salvation itself, the one and only way.

Christ is the only consciousness that is fully awake. Only he can perceive and penetrate to the bottom of the "impossibility" of all things in their sinful, self-enclosed finiteness. Already this finiteness as such brings sorrow to an infinite consciousness, for which the concealing veil of mercy applied to reality by those who mean well is of no avail.

" 'Do you answer nothing?' But Jesus kept silent." Note how God's silence becomes visible before his creatures, above all in the face of their accusations. He does not disentangle the world's contradictions; rather, he overcomes them through silence, even if this means that he has to die (in the hearts that interrogate him). Only when we question him, calling him by his actual name, does he answer us: "I am he."

The beginning and end of Christ's redemptive deed is the spirit of obedience, the bond of union. The beginning is his absolute dependency on the will of the Father ("the Son can do nothing of himself; he can do only what he sees the Father doing", John 5:19). And the end is his total bond with the world and mankind, at whose disposal he has wholly put himself like one who no longer has a self of his own. This begins at the Last Supper, is accomplished when he is nailed to the Cross, and is perfected at the moment of his self-sacrifice. We are astonished by the heights of the mystical graces of an Ignatius, who in the end came to possess permanent open access to the world of the divine. And yet, what becomes evident here in an impressive way is basically what was realized at the institution of the Eucharist.

The man who had been sick for thirty-eight years: God himself comes to the person who cannot come to him through no fault of his own. And whoever appears to be farthest from healing is the first to be healed.

In the parables, Jesus never speaks of his love for us or of his deed of redemption. He describes the King-dom of God in its growth, never making explicit who it was who planted it on earth. The prodigal son returns to his father's home without even giving a hint of who is responsible for the grace of his conver-sion. The Father is always the one who loves and the one who is glorified: this is so in the parables of the merciless servant, of the lord of the vineyard, of the evil vine-dressers, of the great banquet, and so forth. Jesus never said he loves us; he only proved it. Per-haps the great farewell discourse is an exception: here Love speaks "openly, no longer in images", but here the situation is that of the Eucharist: Jesus speaks from the hearts of the disciples who have received him; he speaks to them and, from within them, to the Father. And the Supper is already the beginning of the Passion: the chalice of love has already been poured out, spilled; the farewell discourses are the unrestrained outflowing of the Logos.

If I look down, I see you there kneeling before me, girt with linen and holding the basin: "If I do not wash you, you will not enter into communion with me." If I look in front of me, you are coming toward me with bread and a cup, and, if I should want to steal away, I hear you say: "If you do not eat the flesh of the Son of Man and do not drink his blood, you shall not have life within you." If I look up, I meet your eyes looking down upon me from the Cross, and, if I were to say: "No, Lord, not like this", then I would surely hear: "Away from my sight, adversary; you want to seduce me." You expect us to agree to your sufferings, to say Yes to the heinous things we do to you, have done to you, and will again do. For you want to take us with you into your Passion beyond any possible escape. You so intrude upon us that no other way is left us. But *must* you not in fact do this, since you are Love itself?

The wedding of Cana: Mary has to show our poverty to the Lord—"They have run out of the wine of love." She orders us to fill the stone jars with the clear water of pure readiness, and the Lord transforms the water of nature into the wine of grace. Not *one* little glass of wine results from ten jars of water, but *all* of the water of human life—all man's activity and inactivity, all his sleeping, eating, loving, and dying—everything is taken up into the transformation, and in the end we have the privilege of serving this wine—our best wine, saved up for last—to the Lord.

Je le sens, je n'ai jamais rien fait pour lui. Mais puis-je le regretter? Il a si admirablement tout fait en moi, lui seul, et il me semble qu'il ne veut de moi que l'humilité, et que si je trouvais en moi une seule vertu sur laquelle je puisse reposer les yeux, cela lui déplairait et cela ferait obstacle à son oeuvre: "I feel it deeply: I have never done anything for him. But can I regret this? He has done everything in me so wonderfully, he alone, and it seems to me that the only thing he wants of me is humility, and that, if I were to find in myself one single virtue on which I could rest my eyes, that would displease him and would represent an obstacle to his work." CONSUMMATA

What if the prodigal son were to come home and exclaim: "Father, I have sinned, I am no longer worthy. But I have brought you something from abroad"? With sweet feminine cunning, the woman in the Gospel brought him anointing oil: she did not want to appear before him empty-handed. But her tears show that she did not want to pay him back in installments but all at once. And yet, having nothing, she wanted to give something, in order to demonstrate that she was full of love. She succeeded; therefore we may say that she had calculated correctly; and the Lord sings the praise of this ointment.

The darkest aspect of redemption's dark history is the fact that the deepest and most radical sin first becomes possible only in the light of grace and Christian vision (Hebrews 6). Only a disciple could really betray the Lord. Only here can we measure what the climax of Jesus' sufferings on the Mount of Olives must have been: the Lord's knowledge that, through his Passion, he was pushing sin to its culmination. Hence the proximity of the Church to the Magna Meretrix [or "Great Whore"], a closeness that sometimes makes them indistinguishable. And yet, grace always prevails over all the demonic options of human infidelity.

Au lieu de m'oublier, je ne dois plus penser qu'à lui: "Instead of forgetting myself, what I ought to do is think only of him."   CONSUMMATA

All of our happiness grows out of an immeasurable suffering: the Cross. Is this not an uncanny sort of happiness? Can we possibly just accept it naïvely, or should we not rather attempt to help in acquiring it by some suffering of our own? Should we not at least attempt to receive our happiness from its root, by suffering along with him who merited it for us?[1] But, alas, if we suffer, we only become happy—this

---

[1] The tight original of this sentence can be rendered in English only by periphrasis: *Oder sollten wir versuchen, es uns wenigstens mit-zu-erleiden? Wenigstens von seiner Wurzel her mit-zu-empfangen, im Mit-leiden mit dem, der es uns verdiente?*

again is a gift of his suffering—because, if we suffer, we only become perfected. We cannot, it seems, catch up with God when it comes to suffering, because all of our suffering is already a grace of his own ungraced suffering for us. And so, only one way remains: we must allow ourselves to be overcome by his unsurpassable love.

❖

¡Oh cristalina fuente,
Si en esos tus semblantes plateados,
Formases de repente
Los ojos deseados,
Que tengo en mis entrañas dibujados!

O spring like crystal!
If only, on your silvered-over face,
You would suddenly form
The eyes I have desired,
Which I bear sketched deep within my heart.[2]

JOHN OF THE CROSS

[2] Trans. K. Kavanaugh and O. Rodriguez, *The Collected Works of St. John of the Cross* (Washington, D.C.: ICS Publications, 1973), p. 713.

LOVE

Better perverted love than no love at all: the woman in the Gospel who had sinned out of love is thought worthy of forgiveness, but not the Pharisee, for the simple fact that he had done "nothing".

Il me semble que le coeur pleinement confiant est celui qui, fasciné par la puissance infinie de l'Amour Divin, ne laisse pas les impossibilités humaines limiter son espérance, mais qui donne à sa confiance la taille de l'Amour: "It seems to me that the fully trusting heart is the one that, enthralled by the infinite power of Divine Love, does not allow human impossibilities to limit its hope but gives to its own trust the proportions of Love itself."

CONSUMMATA

Dostoyevsky is wrong when he says that a universal love for man is a false front for egotism, which in this way is avoiding the concrete demands of love. But Nietzsche, too, is wrong when he compares the narrowness of a particular love for those around us with the liberating breadth of a love for those farthest from us. Christ loves in each man the wonderful image of

God, which shines out to him new and unique in each particular case. Thus, his love is at once unbounded and wholly concrete. This would not be the case if he were to love the individual either aesthetically, on account of his particularity, or communistically, only on the basis of his common human nature.

Awe is more transcendent than longing. The latter possesses only its own measure; the former, precisely by stepping back, can measure the distance from the Beloved and therefore also his actual proximity. Longing can only make immanence swell beyond its proper bounds; awe brings the transcendent into the immanent.

We are not asked; we are invited.

"The lover assumes that love exists in the heart of the other person; precisely this assumption allows him to build up love in the other starting from the bottom. An architect does not think very highly of the stones and rubble he needs for the construction; a teacher presupposes ignorance; a disciplinarian, unruly ways. But the lover who is busy building up knows only one procedure: he must presuppose the existence of love. Supposing that the lover should succeed in building up love in another person: when the edifice is finally complete, then the lover will stand apart by himself and with shame say to himself: I always knew that this existed!" KIERKEGAARD

And yet we must contrast this statement of Kierke-gaard's with Scheler's thought that true love does not see value in the beloved but creates it. Or, in a better formulation: he discloses it creatively. For what could be creative if not love? But Kierkegaard is just as right: How could love ever ascribe a work to itself? As always, the solution lies in Christ: foundering in his awareness that he could not awaken the love of the world, his vessel shattered in the abyss of his deed's uselessness (in the words of Albert Schweitzer)—but then his fragrance came to fill the whole world, and the water of the Spirit flowed forth from him and passed over into our own hearts.

The giving of external gifts is never essential in love; it is but a makeshift measure that aims at abolishing the self by filling up the inequalities and dividing distances between oneself and the other. Only when there is no longer anything left to give but love itself will love have attained its full maturity.

When an object becomes a symbol for the person— and in love this occurs continually—then the object can move us to tears. What is moving here is the helplessness of love, which must conceal itself in such garments. But precisely the distance between love itself and its concealing cover makes love emerge all the more nakedly, so to speak. This is the secret attraction of the symbolic, as such, in art and most especially in Sacred Scripture.

The most sublime thing that human beings can give one another is an occasion for love and awe.

To our anxious question: "Do I love God?", Scripture responds with the counterquestion: "Do you love your neighbor?" "If a person does not love his brother, whom he sees, how can he love God, whom he does not see?" One thing is thus certain: no one may turn to the love of God out of disappointment with human love. Such a person would be subject to Péguy's judgment: *Parce qu'ils n'aiment rien, ils croient qu'ils aiment Dieu*: "Because they love nothing, they think they love God." But does human love suffice to assure us of the love of God? If it is a selfless, self-surrendering love, then God is not far. "Beloved, let us love one another, for love comes from God." The two are one; anyone who has begun to love will realize this. Both of them demand the same effort, the same painful fidelity; both raise us far above a neat balance between giving and taking. The same flame burns in the foundation of all Being: whoever has felt it can no longer live for anything else.

It is a wonderful thing that among friends many things can be passed over in silence without this disturbing their mutual understanding. Between spouses this is more difficult.

"A reversible relation at times takes place between persons that, on both sides, is a relationship to the infinite. On the one hand, it is the beloved who, in every expression of love on the lover's part, lovingly recognizes the immeasurable element. On the other hand, it is the lover who senses this immeasurableness, because he recognizes that love's debt is infinite. Here, one and the same thing is, at the same time, infinitely great and infinitely small. The beloved admits with love that the lover does infinitely more through the smallest deed than all others can do with even the greatest sacrifices. And the lover admits to himself that, despite all possible sacrifices, he remains infinitely far behind what he recognizes as his debt. What a wonderful balance is accomplished here by the infinite!"   KIERKEGAARD

The rocket: steeply does love's fiery ray shoot up to heaven, stop, and burst (at the moment of ecstasy), and a thousand sparks stream ever more quickly down to earth. God sends you, torn and divided, back to your brethren.

❖

Where there is infidelity, love was never present. Where there is fidelity, love does not yet necessarily exist. The heart can say: "Even if I cannot love you, I want at least to be faithful to you." But the bond of fidelity either leads to love or contains deep within itself, unknown to feeling, the knot of love, which is tied outside of time.

The "easy way" (*voie facile*) of Little Thérèse is genuine for the simple reason that it so refutes for all time all false concepts of "heroic virtue". God and the measure of love that he fans into flame within a soul: only these are ever truly extraordinary. God is no trainer of souls bent on attaining extravagant record performances. He is a Lover who wants nothing but great love and who accepts with a smile everything such a love invents to offer him. But he declines everything man uses—no matter how subtly—to put on airs before him.

True love always springs more from the vision of the beloved's love-worthiness than from one's inner impulse to love. The latter, all by itself, would lead only to an exhibition, for the other person's benefit, of one's own ability to love, and this would be a magical action rather than an act of love.

❖

It is not difficult to understand the unity of love for God and love for man. We have only to grasp the fact that love is not enjoyment and a feeling of fusion but an act of devotion, whereby the lover puts his heart at the beloved's service. In order to love God we do not have to renounce the love of the world but only its disordered enjoyment. Temperance and love are not only "compatible": temperance so much belongs to the inner essence of love that, according

84

to Paul, the person who loves keeps all the commandments. And he does so unconsciously. The negativity of prohibitions has been transcended by the loving person into the positivity of love: *ama et fac quod vis* [love and do what you will].

In the parable of the Good Samaritan, the answer does not fit the question. The question was: "Who is my *neighbor* [literally, the person 'closest' to me]? To whom should I do good?" And at the end Christ asks: "Which of the three was 'neighbor' to the man fallen among thieves?" Answer: The one who showed him compassion. Moral: Go and do the same. This means, in the first place, that the question asked can have only a *practical* answer, while the theoretical question had been an evasion on the part of the man who "wanted to justify himself". In the second place, all "closeness" has to be first *created* by love.

The great "vicious circle" in the Gospel. On the one hand: "Whoever has my commandments and keeps them is the one who loves me." On the other hand: "Whoever has love has fulfilled the Law." Here no one can say what is cause and what effect. No one may reduce one statement to the other. No one (this is what it would amount to) may construct a system rationalizing the relationship between nature and grace.

The multiplication of loaves as a symbol not only of the love of God but also of the love of neighbor: multiplication by lavish squandering is the natural image of every true love. In the end we collect infinitely more than was there at the beginning, even after the nourishing bread has long been consumed. Here Jesus is illustrating through a miracle the law of the seed that dies and rises again.

The fact that God became man has once again made the paths from man to man passable without danger. Previously, did not the highest kind of human relationship have to renounce the carnal aspect? Now, however, after the Incarnation, the relationship of man and woman has become a sacramental symbol for that between God and man (1 Corinthians 11, Ephesians 5). And so the carnal relationship can now become transfigured, to its very foundation, within the reality of the Mystical Body of Christ. The necessary Christian distance of reverence from one another—"you are temples of the Most High"—at the same time means the overcoming of the tragic distance conditioned by sin. The Eucharist is the *Body* of Christ, and in this Body we are one.

"My kind of sensibility experienced a great sorrow when, after committing serious errors, I received graces from God—a far greater sorrow than if he had punished me. Indeed, I believe that a single such grace devastated, shamed, and distressed me more than if I had had to endure many illnesses and numerous other sufferings." TERESA OF AVILA

Everything human remains suspended; nothing human ought to become entrenched and hardened. Just think of the relationship between lovers: if he himself loves, the beloved does not take in order to have, in order to become rich, but because it is the lover's joy to give. But the lover himself would like to enrich the beloved through his gift: he does not give in order himself to enjoy the giving of it. Therefore, in order to gratify the lover (in order to give his gift back to him), the receiver accepts it in such a way that he really finds himself enriched and shows it. Whoever finds this too abstract should read the conclusion of the Letter to the Philippians. There, Paul actually lives out before us this dialectic of love in the most lovely manner.

La volonté n'aime qu'en voulant aimer: "The will loves only by willing to love." FRANCIS DE SALES

In our dealings with God, we must act "as if" we loved. Both affectively and effectively we must "imitate" lovers. This is not hypocrisy but simply the result of the fact that we live by faith and not by vision (or by feeling or knowing). This unique principle of concealment is what sets the love of God apart from every other love. It is the more difficult because love wants proofs: it wants to find its repose in its vision of a direct answer. But it is also easier, because precisely here the soul may (and must) renounce the evidence of its own love; easier also because the natural gravitation of the soul toward God continues in force; we are guaranteed perpetual access to God and shelter in him; we are assured that our love will always be reciprocated by him and undisturbed by lower impulses; and we are assured of the indestructible fidelity of God.

L'amour pur [pure love] does not exclude the thought of being rewarded. Love rejoices over the "reward" and the prospect of being united forever with the beloved. But love is not based on reward as a necessary condition. Already in the natural realm, as Scheler's ethic of values has shown, the will aims primarily at value, not at pleasure. Pleasure is the "reward" of the realization of values, not its goal, except in the case where pleasure is sought for its own sake as an autonomous value. On the other hand, Thomas Aquinas insisted on the natural unity of value and reward: their separation results in puritanism (witness Kant) and destroys nature. It could well happen that, for pedagogic reasons, God conceals for a given time the aspect of pleasure and reward, in order to test the purity of love. This, however, is far from giving man the right to construct an ethical system based on a dichotomy of value and reward, as Kant has done.

❖

"Dryness, drowsiness. Since my Beloved deigns to slumber, I shall not disturb him. I am overjoyed that he does not treat me like a stranger and stand on ceremony with me."   THÉRÈSE OF LISIEUX

❖

"The less one seeks oneself in the Beloved, the greater the pleasure flowing from union with the Beloved."

MEISTER ECKHART

In the Gospel, the thought of a reward is counterbalanced by Christ's statement that to him who has, more shall be given, so that he becomes exceedingly rich, and that from him who has not, even that which he has shall be taken from him. This means that no equilibrium at all applies here. The explanation is that a person who has (love) seeks nothing else (than becoming nothing). He knows no happiness other than love itself.

Harmony without melody is like sexuality without love. Sex is the rustle of a harp accompanying a pure voice. Without this voice, sex is senseless, repulsive: Wagner.

❖

Homosexuality is so ruinous because here man has caught sight of his own beauty and made it into an object. If the male is involved, he has likewise objectivized his God-willed superiority. No being, as a matter of fact, should enmesh himself in the love that

89

seeks full satisfaction in beauty, which a special grace graciously conceals from him.

"Love your beloved wife faithfully and ardently, but—if you have found one another in God—love of neighbor should be the consecration of your union. Love your friend sincerely and devotedly, but—if you have found one another in God—love of neighbor should be what you learn from one another."

KIERKEGAARD

One of the most difficult things for a believer to do is to help a doubter. Like Moses, when he spoke to the people, we must cover our face so as to dim the radiance of the evidence within us and so, according to Paul's words, mourn with those who mourn, question with those who question, and doubt with those who doubt; for these will overcome their distrust of splendor only in this muted light. At the same time, however, we must let through enough brightness so that the faint-hearted will gather courage and derive strength from the example of faith. In other words, we must be the *way* and at the same time the *goal*, which is possible only because Christ became both things for *us* simultaneously. For his vitality consists in this: that he always stands at the level of the person he is educating and yet always is to be found as well at [as!] the final goal of his education. He walks along with the disciples toward Emmaus; but as they walk they discover that he is already reposing in the assurance of the goal. He is the Way, yet also the Truth, and, for that very reason, the Life.

Christ's love possesses the utmost tact. It knows how to combine the most intense demands with the most exquisite unobtrusiveness.

Amour pur and *musique pure*. When listening to pure music one is "all ears", while with programmatic music or any music with a specific purpose, a degree of reflection enters in: an enjoyment of the enjoyment, or a shared enjoyment of the "meaning" or "experience" that underlies it. Thus, too, pure love is pure objectivity: the beloved is the exclusive object; the lover himself does not also figure as object, either indirectly or reflexively. Against this thought it could be objected, to be sure, that God, the highest object, is no mere object but, concurrently, Love itself: as such, he always also encompasses and delights the subject. However, even when he is infused into our souls as Holy Spirit, God is never "my life". Rather, even my subjective love is also taken up into his objective Being and, as it were, suspended there. Within the unity of the act of love itself there is to be found the distance between my infinitely unimportant contribution and the Holy Spirit's act of love in me. And, thus, the distance to "my" love is once again restored.

The highest earthly love is like the harmony of two

persons making music together. The solitary sounds each produces meet in a third dimension, blend together into unity in the medium of ether, and thus, as an objective construct, are given back to both of them within their individual hearing. And if the hands of the players should accidentally touch on the keyboard: what has this to do with that union realized as a grace beyond them both, in God?

When God demands of us something difficult, we often seek to be aided in our compliance by motives that rob the action of its whole value. For instance, we try to convince ourselves that what is sacrificed—friends, a comfortable life, and so on—at bottom means little to us. What if God should give us only what no longer has any value for *him*?

The arrogant person is like a black object. In order to acquire some energy and thus be able to "shine", he sucks up all light into himself, not knowing that precisely because of this he no longer reflects a single ray and so is wholly darkness. The humble person is already bright: whatever he receives he passes on, and he "shines" precisely because he doesn't clutch at things. Because he readily transmits the borrowed light that falls on him, he himself becomes light. Love and mission are one.

Perfect hope must be based on love, that is, on possibly having to disregard the "fulfillment" of the relationship of love, which in this life always remains a formal one.

❖

Every love wants the beloved to act—above all, God's love, in which we who have been redeemed are apparently nothing but beings who are acted upon.

❖

The edifying principle in Protestantism rests on a process of downward leveling: before God and from the divine perspective, all human activity, all so-called religion, is nothing but idle sin and inanity. For man, the only genuine humility that saves is for him to acknowledge this and cling exclusively to God's grace. The edifying principle in Catholicism rests on this: that the omnipotence of grace is so great that it can take into account even man's powerless striving, and that, although God does everything, still this never happens without man.

❖

"Because God is Love, it can come to pass through love that what each individual has becomes the common possession of all. For, when someone loves in another what he himself does not have, then he too comes to possess it in the other" (Augustine). We should take such a thought much to heart, considering the drive of some to pile up personal merits. Should we not rather desire to be good in order to afford joy to others in heaven, if not already on earth? If we were to find our joy as we should, in the beauty of God and of his saints, then we would be rich, much richer than with personal merits. Humanly speaking, we could say that a very particular happiness would belong to the poorest person in heaven who lived solely on the beauty of others, wholly at love's expense, like those poor people who can be delighted by everything without coveting it. But this is just the point: it is the saints who are made this way—their poverty shall be their wealth, and through their bareness God will shine most brightly. This is why they will possess more of what is God's and be able to communicate more of him to others. In this and no other way will God be all in all.

"Often it seems that—although self-love is the most damnable thing—man nevertheless does not have enough strength to be alone with self-love. It can only really manifest itself when another 'I' is found, and then the two can find the strength in their bond for them to feel their reality in self-love. If anyone should think he has found Christian love because he has fallen in love or found a friend, he would be trapped in a great error. Wherever the Christian principle is found, there too is self-denial; it is the essential form of Christianity. By contrast, wherever the Christian principle is not found, there an inebriation of self-esteem is the highest value, and the apex of this inebriation is what is admired. Love and friendship, moreover, are precisely the peak of self-esteem: it is the 'I' drunk with the other 'I'. The more tightly and intimately these two 'I's become bound together into one 'I', the more selfishly does this unified self shut itself off from all others."   KIERKEGAARD

❖

To allow oneself truly to be loved is more difficult than for oneself to love, and more humility is required. First of all, one is an object and not an autonomously acting subject, and hence one must have the humility to receive instead of to give. Then, too, a total and quite complex purification of one's interior veracity is necessary. Considerable time is required between the discovery that one can oneself love and the discovery that one can truly be loved without one's lover being blinded by some illusion. It is easy to find oneself love-worthy with arrogance; but this does not satisfy a person who is loved and does not want to hide any part of his truth from the person loving him. He will mostly turn his glance away from himself with shame in order *not* to discover what is good about himself and direct that glance toward the lover alone, in whose eyes—and nowhere else—he would like to glimpse the reflection of his own goodness: "If he finds it good to love me, there must be something to it. . . . But that, thank God, does not concern me. . . ." This shame contains an important truth; but it should not be based on the certainty of having a fuller knowledge than the other, of knowing with certainty, that is, that this other "sees too much in oneself" or that "he doesn't know all." Both things would be a distrust of his love, the suspicion that it is not absolute but conditioned and dependent on a certain number of qualities. Here the only help comes from a humble and loving trust in the rightness of every love, which defies all justification and which, even if it by chance does not "know everything", still is infinitely more knowing and clairvoyant than an egotistical self-hatred. In the end, all true love is not blind: it alone really sees, but, seeing, it overlooks and thus banishes guilt from the world. Therefore, let others love in you the good things God has given you and do not deprive love of its nourishment.

The rejection of self-love by Protestants belongs to their depreciation of secondary causes. But in this way they stop up the wellspring of joy and all human activity.

To love oneself in God, as a gift bequeathed to us by him. To love oneself with the same reverence—and to help build up and beautify the temple of the Holy Spirit in us with the same painstaking devotion—as we would employ in any other act of divine service.

Les personnes qui ne s'aiment que par charité, comme le prochain, se supportent charitablement sans se flatter, comme on supporte le prochain dans ses imperfections: "People who love themselves only out of charity, as they love their neighbor, bear with themselves charitably and without flattery, just as one bears with one's neighbor and his imperfections."   FÉNELON

"We could say that God accepts with love the demands of love. Through his love for another person, the lover contracts an infinite debt—a debt also with regard to God as the guardian of his beloved. At this point all comparisons become impossible, and love has permanently found its Master."   KIERKEGAARD

There exists a jealousy with regard to God: that he can better love and more deeply possess a person whom we love and would like to possess, that he can see him from within beyond all concealment and accept his fullness of surrender.

Eros and Agape are neither identical nor contrary. For Eros is capable of understanding the meaning of Agape and subordinating itself to it by undergoing a death and a resurrection.

Christian love culminates in the power to draw back from one's beloved for God's sake, when one becomes an obstacle to that person or when one shuts off his vision of God. Then it can be the greatest love to allow oneself to be "hated" in order to restore freedom to the beloved. Even the Lord himself wants to be loved solely in the will and the Person of the Father. "Away from me, Satan!" said he to the same Peter whom he had just declared blessed.

"To help another person come to love God is to love him; and to be supported by another person in loving God is to be loved." KIERKEGAARD

Believing he was damned, Francis de Sales exclaimed: *Quoi qu'il en soit, Seigneur, si je ne puis vous aimer en l'autre vie, puisque personne ne vous loue en enfer, que du moins je mette à profit pour vous aimer tous les moments de ma courte existence ici-bas*: "Whatever may be the case, O Lord: if I cannot love you in the other life, since no one praises you in hell, let me at least spend in loving you every moment of my short existence here on earth."

It isn't right that we should have to overlook the beauty and, more generally, all the worth of the world in order to love God in them. The lover finds his beloved's house and garden all the lovelier when she is present in them: he loves them for his beloved's sake, and his beloved in them, and he is not blind to anything that relates to her.

"Here, the deeper the wound, the more richly health blossoms." JOHN OF THE CROSS

In my soul Christ seeks the will of the Father and the Father seeks the image of the Son. When both of them meet there, my soul is full of the Holy Spirit.

Francis de Sales' wonderful parable: A rich man fetches a musician to play for him. At first the lord listens to the musician with kind attention. Then he goes off hunting and leaves him at home playing by himself. But the musician's love is not yet fully pure, for he still listens to his own playing and takes pleasure in it. In the end he becomes deaf and plays only to render "service". Now obedience and pure love coincide.

❖

Les plaies du coeur ont cela qu'elles peuvent être sondées jusqu'au fond, pourvu qu'on ait le courage de les pénétrer: "Wounds of the heart have this about them: they can be probed to the bottom provided one has the courage to penetrate them." BOSSUET

LIFE

Non eloquimur magna, sed vivimus: "We [Christians] do not speak great things, but we live them."

MINUTIUS FELIX

Nos obligations ne sont point acquittées que nous n'ayons payé jusqu'à l'être et à la substance: "Our obligations have not been met until we have paid for our very being itself and our substance."   CONDREN

An asceticism and mysticism based on the natural longing for the vision of God (*desiderium naturale visionis*) would be anthropocentric: the standard and the goal would be derived from man himself—his longing, his eros, his self-fulfillment, in short, his own perfection. By contrast, a theocentric asceticism and mysticism would have as their point of departure man's creatureliness and its fundamental exigencies: the praise and service of God, reverential awe before the absolute Lord, and obedience to him. On this basis, all norms are to be found in God's hand from the outset. Here we can see that the way of distance and awe is the shortest way to attain to pure love.

But, on the opposite side of things, whoever would jump over the level of "nature" in order to start at once with "Christian" sublimity will most likely be importing the unconscious concupiscence of nature into the highest level of reality.

The most perfect phonograph record is the one that cannot be recognized as record when it is being played. So, too, the most perfect person. But he succeeds in becoming this only when he does not aim at his own perfection but at that of the music he wants to relay.

Humility is not a virtue but the realization that we lack every virtue. And, when we call it the "foundation of all virtues", we should carefully see whether anything can be "built" on such a realization or, above all, whether "virtues" can be erected on it. The Gospel is no "school of virtue", in the sense of classical antiquity, but a school of God's service. This is something different, even if exteriorly both things can often be confused.

The ideal of the idealist is to forge ahead with reflection until he reaches the crystalline world of necessity, of the idea. The ideal of the Christian is the reverse: to look away from himself, to overlook himself by looking at God. On this road God will surely not spare him insight into himself; but even this will be the opposite of idealistic reflection. Hegel's demonic aspect consists in his having equated Christian re-flection with philosophical reflection, or indeed in his having sought to empty the former of value in favor of the latter.

To accomplish a "revaluation of all (ascetical) val-ues": instead of a table of values based on "possess-ing", we would have to have one based on "withstanding" ("with-standing" in the sense of "standing before someone", and in such a way that we with-stand or stand-over *whatever* stands before us). The first table refers everything to my own per-fection; the second refers everything to the situation between two persons.

The experience of our sinfulness: how everything that *could* be pure and pleasing in the sight of God—indeed, even the most innocent and ordinary thing—is vitiated by the breath of unholiness, as when a per-son who has foul breath exhales it even when he sleeps. *Nihil est innoxium* ["nothing is harmless", says the Pentecost hymn *Veni, sancte Spiritus*]. This is how we could understand Luther's and Kant's concept of "radical evil". And yet, it would be a weakness to stop here and not plunge even this thought into God's grandeur. Here precisely is where we must perceive the opportunity to leap out of ourselves: as when in prayer we recognize, for instance, that no act of pure praise will ever rise from our soul and that the best love it is capable of is still full of egotism and all manner of stains. At such a moment we must awaken in ourselves a longing for the great purifying fire that would of itself consume us so that we might at last adore with all our soul. But at the same time we must perform an act of obedience and continue in this foul pit for as long as God deems it a good thing.

Evil can deceive us with a convincing "realism": in its light, all things appear close up and stripped, in the true-to-life clarity of *verismo*, rescued from that blurry and hazy atmosphere that they have on "good" days. And yet the former is the illusion and the latter the truth: grace envelops our soul and our destiny in thin veils; in the light of faith our real contours should indeed be hazy. A Christian existence without this atmosphere is as abstract as a surrealistic painting.

To be sure, evil can show us our weaknesses very clearly: this is why those temptations are allowed. But only the person who projects this experience back onto the landscape of grace possesses the right perspective and has made the correct use of the experience.

How wonderful that Jesus listens to the prayer of the unbelieving Thomas, although he rejects the necessity of the test by experience that Thomas proposes. When we are granted a miracle we have been expecting, according to Pascal and Bloy, what we should learn from it is the preeminence of naked, unsupported faith.

The dialectic of humility: Ignatius exacts humility from his men so that they will be pleasing to both God and men. Without amiability there is no apostolate, and, without humility, no amiability. Humility can be used as a means when it is found already at the root of our movement of search.

On fait insensiblement de la piété un certain métier, dans lequel on veut réussir comme dans les autres: "Without intending to, we turn piety into a sort of profession in which we would like to succeed as in any other."

NICOLE

To strive for one's own perfection is a bourgeois ideal. The bourgeois social climber must concentrate on getting ahead in the world. He must also see to it that no one denies his person the honor owed it. In him there is always a residue of ambition and the fear of again falling from the platform he has so laboriously climbed. The noble person knows nothing of all this because his honor does not primarily depend on his person but on his family. Nor does he represent himself but his family. The bourgeois, on the contrary, represents himself: he stands and falls with himself. This is why the striving for one's own perfection is a bourgeois ideal. Now, what God wants from every soul is a noble and not a bourgeois mentality. He desires service and a sense of service. He desires that each soul should make his will its own and renounce its own will. And those serving are not concerned if, as a result of their service, their own perfection increases. For them perfection coincides with the goodness of service well rendered.

Representation, according to Przywara, sums up the essence of the Catholic principle with both great mystery and great precision: Trinity, Incarnation, redemption, Church, sacraments, the ethical norm of Catholic life. . . . A sense for representation, therefore, remains the best endowment for grasping and appropriating this Catholic essence.

The ethos of representation is noble; the ethos of self-fulfillment by the person is bourgeois. The sense for rank and subordination is noble; the idea of individuals' equality of value and rights is bourgeois. The ethos of distance as respect for the other and as an abiding form of love is noble; the ethos of closeness through a "personal" relationship of familiarity and the ideal of the greatest possible directness is bourgeois. The ethos of service is noble; bourgeois is the ethos of virtue as a moral "accomplishment", a task to be carried out, the "striving for perfection". Noble is the conviction that self-abandonment and self-sacrifice belong to the very nature of things; but bourgeois is the art of the safeguard, the mercantile instinct that ventures a sacrifice only for the sake of a greater gain (one does not like to let go of something acquired with much effort). Noble is the ideal that remains upwardly open; bourgeois is the drive to plan and establish everything once and for all ("so far will I go, and no farther"). Noble is an unexamined and naïve self-assurance: one knows one contains a mystery; bourgeois is the wavering between fear and self-conceit: one's worth must continually be affirmed by others, and the conventions of reciprocal esteem are of paramount importance. Noble is a religious attitude that, through thick and thin, clings to the golden thread of divine pleasure and that, through all the circumstances of the religious experience, knows how to feel its way to the final iota of this purely formal divine will; bourgeois is a religious destiny made up of a series of interior catastrophes, because God is so ready to give his grace that he smashes all the houses of cards man is ever building with his ideals and plans and pushes all false familiarity back to the necessary distance.

Every person bears within himself the aptitude for both things: to be a narrow-souled bourgeois and a philistine (this is what he is as a human being with a corrupt nature) or to be a saint (this is what grace destines him to be). God can transform us from one kind of person into the other. The social categories here provide only a metaphor, but admittedly a very eloquent metaphor.

A truth has full resonance only when proclaimed out of the fullness of a lived tradition one has made one's own.

In the disciples we see only one predominant flaw emerge: their spiritual arrogance, or better, their carnal arrogance in spiritual matters. At all costs they want the first places in the Kingdom of Heaven, that is, they want to be the most perfect. All their ideas are focused on this desire. In vain does the Lord fight against this incarnation of original sin in them: it is as if they were deaf to his teachings. Until at last the Cross converts them and shatters their ladders to heaven. In the narratives of their encounters with the Risen Lord, we see that their dream of virtue has been exhausted; in its place Pentecost inserts the burning sting of mission.

Just as the phonograph needle follows the subtlest, least visible undulations of the record, so too should the soul obey the Holy Spirit. Not to jump from the track, not to want to play any other music, not to skip any prescribed repetition *dal capo* . . . in any event, the symphony is soon over.

Two kinds of humility. Humility that sees: for this kind, humility is truth; it can see its own nothingness and the fact that grace is everything. And then humility that does not see, or chooses not to see: to it the motto of Francis de Sales applies: *voir sans regarder*— "to see without looking at", namely, one's own goodness, the flaws of others. But both kinds belong together.

Con-sol-ation. As a blind man feels the sun [*sol*] without seeing it, so does the soul feel God.

"Whenever we undertake, carry out, and complete a good work, each of us has had the experience of feeling joy one time but not the next. One time we know how to seize such joy, and the next time we do not. We thus learn that knowing and enjoying do not spring from our own abilities but from God's grace. In this way we are healed of the pride of our own choices."   AUGUSTINE

Nothing plays a greater role in God's pedagogical art than the shift from one to the other extreme. No sooner have we learned something half-way and begun to grasp it than (oh, shock!) out of the warm bath and into the cold! This is meant to ensure that we do not settle into any situation but remain pliable, and to make us recognize that true insight does not come from what we have grasped but from ever-greater readiness and deeper obedience.

Je sens que plus je serai effacée, plus je serai rayonnante. Lorsqu'on a réellement conscience que les sources d'eau vive n'ont jailli que sous l'impulsion de l'Esprit Saint donnée dans les mérites de Jésus-Christ, on ne pense qu'à faciliter le cours autant qu'on peut, afin que la semence divine produise son maximum de rendement pour la gloire du Père. Retenir pour soi la moindre chose sous prétexte de modestie,

*ce serait un manque d'humilité autant que de largeur et de
liberté. Lorsqu'on ne possède rien en propre, on ne se ferme
pas par modestie. N'as-tu jamais rencontré de ces affiches
sur lesquelles on peut lire ces mots: «exproprié pour cause
d'utilité publique»?*: "I feel that the more I vanish the
more resplendent I will be. When we know in our
bones that the springs of living water have shot up in
us only under the impulse of the Holy Spirit, be-
stowed by virtue of the merits of Jesus Christ, then
we can think only of helping the flow along as best
we can, so that the divine seed will yield its maximum harvest for the glory of the Father. To hold
back the slightest thing for ourselves under pretext of
modesty would be a lack of humility as well as of
generosity and freedom. When you possess nothing
of your own, you do not close yourself off for reasons
of modesty. Have you never seen those signs that an-
nounce: 'confiscated for the public good'?"

CONSUMMATA

Benedixit, fregit, deditque [He blessed, broke, and gave]:
Because he blessed, he broke, and because he broke
you, he was able to bestow you as gift.

"And he will lead you where you do not want to
go." Lord, lead me there. I would like to go where I
do not want to go.

Voluntary self-humbling usually contains a few grains
of arrogance, but not for that reason should we shun

it, for it is one way to genuine, involuntary humbling by God.

Over and over again we are faced with our inability, our incapacity: we struggle to reach God, but in vain. But then, when we are exhausted—precisely in the midst of this exhaustion, this failure—we experience that it is he who has come to us. Exhaustion as the "rustling sound" in which God is to be found (Elijah!). How could weakness be an obstacle? Weak armies are easily defeated, weak fortresses easily overrun, provided they are smart enough to capitulate. Otherwise they are also stormed, but not before they have been shot to pieces, much to their own detriment. In conclusion: learn how to surrender!

Effacement, une vie effacée [self-effacement, a life in the wings]. This word describes the essence of humility, which, while not exactly obliterated or wiped out, has nonetheless become invisible to itself and to others—permeable, apparently inefficient and unreal, and yet for that very reason all the more efficacious.

We spend a whole life long awaiting the arrival of the extraordinary person, instead of transforming the ordinary people around us into such.

"If a person thinks that what he drinks should benefit only himself, then no living water will spring forth from his breast. But if he hastens to bring help to his neighbor, then his wellspring does not dry up, because it is intent on flowing."   AUGUSTINE

What appears to be virtue is often nothing but the result of two opposed vices that, in their contrary orientation, cancel each other out. We recognize this especially when we try to combat one of them: immediately the other gains power. Above all, those virtues we think we possess "by nature" and the humanistic virtues of the "golden mean" most probably are often based on this illusion.

Affective prayer is very often a ruse whereby man evades the challenge of listening to God's will: we drown God's sober demands under a flood of noisy expectations, until his voice becomes inaudible. Long prayers are likewise often a flight from the minute present instant in which God really makes himself understood by the soul.

The Christian endeavor is so difficult, among other things, because nature tends to black out awareness and switch to "automatic pilot". (This is the grain of truth contained in pragmatism.) From the perspective of grace, by contrast, we seem to incur guilt if for even one moment we cease to be awake, watching for the Word that is speaking to us unceasingly and in an ever-new way. Being awake is a fundamental demand of the Lord's parables, and this means a continual readiness to receive the unexpected, to embrace things we have not learned by rote.

What manners! To receive God's daily visit not in the living room of one's soul but in the kitchen or the hallway!

The kiss of Judas. How often we abuse God's love in the presence of bystanders: "Just see on what good terms I stand with him! I can even kiss him!"

The experience of feeling our powerlessness to reach God always contains as well an indication of the way on which we would surely find God—if only we had enough courage and strength to start walking.

You chose it because it is hard. I want to choose it because you chose it. But I do not say: "I want to choose it because it is hard." For to choose what you have chosen is easy, even if it is hard.

Two ways from the self to God. In the case of some persons, above all the least complex, the self can simply become transparent. The creature's natural attitude, its disappearance before the Creator, is discovered in a very naïve manner. With most of us, however, the opposition of the "dark tyrant" within us is so powerful that this self must slowly be broken up to the last grain, like a rock under the continual attack of the waves. It must crumble away, rot, burn up, until the way is finally open. And the greatest opposition comes from spiritual aspirations.

Very few people have been struck by the unspeakable beauty of the figure of Abraham. The sublime thing about him, as always in the Old Testament, lies in the fact that a highly personal destiny becomes through and through a likeness of a completely different destiny—Christ's. Abraham's distance from and his proximity to Christ, in their inextricable interwovenness, constitute what, in the purest sense, is edifying about him. Thus, the sacrifice of Isaac is a symbolic high point of the Old Covenant with the God of justice, for whom all animal sacrifices are but substitutes for the human sacrifice owed him. At the same time, however, it is also a culminating likeness for God's very deed of redemption in the New Testament: the immolation of his Son. But this New Covenant is equally prefigured in the turning away of the knife. Once these two aspects are connected, an infinite perspective results, as in a hall of mirrors.

"The saint's existence among us is not abolished; and yet he will have to stake out new encampments for his spirit. Or, if he cannot make up his mind to do this, it may well be that for him there has once more arrived the time of peregrination, which makes available to him (for whom renown is so incongruous) the countless possibilities to infiltrate enjoyed by a seeming insignificance."   RILKE

114

Christ's demand (in the meditation on the Two Standards in the *Exercises* of Ignatius) that we embrace poverty and relinquish all honors as a way to the third stage, that of humility, is the demand that we give practical external expression to what is already the factual condition of our interior being. Visible poverty is the practical portrayal of our factual impoverishment through sin; dishonor is the external truth of our interior disgrace. This is exactly why they are the way of humility: they are the truthful acknowledgment of our interior as it is before God.

"Saint Francis: that is already a great deal. . . . But since his time money has become spiritual—an element that soars and ventures far beyond the category of tangible possessions, something almost independent of its possessor, an atmosphere without any possible contrast. The task now is to find a new poverty as counterpart to this new type of 'wealth', all of which has now retreated far into the realm of the invisible. We can always pretend, through external imitation, that we are poor; but real poverty must be born anew in the soul, and there will probably be nothing Franciscan about it."   RILKE

"Essential existence is interiority, and the interiority of the acting person is suffering."   KIERKEGAARD

Many Christians (especially Protestants) are like beggars who are continually knocking at doors. Time and again they hear a friendly "Come in!", but they do not enter because they feel that "beggars belong in the street." Perhaps they are afraid they will not be able to behave with enough refinement in an elegant house. Permission to enter is always a humiliation as well.

Dieu immole des parties, dont je ne connaissais même pas l'existence. Je vois que je jouissais de certaines fibres, seulement maintenant que j'en suis privée: "God is sacrificing parts of me that I did not even know existed. Only now that I have been deprived of them do I realize that I used to enjoy certain fibers of my being."

CONSUMMATA

O You who heal us by wounding us! Who heal us from the madness of totality, from the pestilence of invulnerability.

There are people to whom God applies little containers like those attached to the wounds of the rubber tree. From time to time he collects them in order to process the yield. How mysterious, this industry of redemption, how impenetrable to our understanding!

"The final eradication of faults takes place with the same means that, legend tells us, was used to kill the

Hydra—the monster whose heads always grew back with increase. She had to be destroyed with fire."

SURIN

A person who looks for pity from others in matters of the soul is degrading himself too easily. But before God, too, there exists something like a masochism of the soul—notwithstanding the fact that our prayer can never and should never be anything other than a beggar's plea. And this masochism consists in a false despair and a contemptuous self-degradation. Little Thérèse said: "There are things we keep silent about even before God."

It is not true, thank God, that all prayers and promises are untrue and deceitful that afterward are not kept or turned into a deed, no more than those blossoms are untrue that do not turn into fruit. The act of blossoming possesses a meaning and a value in itself, which may indeed include the tendency toward fructification but which, as a prerequisite for it, bears a particular worth of its own. Therefore, we ought not to suppress our own blossoming only because not everything will turn to fruit in the autumn. Allowing storm and hail to do their work belongs to human discretion.

Lives of saints are so monotonous and insipid either because one doesn't let the saints speak for themselves or because they themselves often cannot speak. Many of them lack the means of expression, and so they return time and again to the relief provided by the Song of Songs, or they cling to a traditional schema that supports their expressive wings but camouflages what is most personal about their experience. Only a few have not only spoken but actually expressed *themselves*. And these few—who knows of them?

Most preachers keep to abstractions because, in the final analysis, they are afraid that one of their listeners will actually take something concrete seriously and put it into practice, here and now. Rhetoric is the compensation for the fact that the absolute does not appear possible. The preacher knows in advance, as it were, that he is a useless servant, and, in order at least to appear to be useful, he does "everything"— everything that can be done in this way. And this same sense of despair is also the source of the endless stream of moralizing that flows from the pulpit. But we should remember that morality is to Christian truth as matter is to life.

No hard-and-fast rule applies to the role played in the Christian relationship to God by the human relaxation afforded by art, nature, fellowship, and so forth. There are times when God demands our unconditional effort, and then we must walk quickly through the streets without stopping to window-shop. But there are also times when God himself indicates that diversions are in order, and it would then be false for the Christian to enjoy God's gifts with a bad conscience. A good conscience in enjoyment could even be a measure of the fact that a person is not being more meticulous about himself than God desires.

❖

Every description of mysticism must start with the insight that God's ways with souls cannot be reduced to a system. The experiences of Teresa of Avila, for instance, are wholly individual and not even particularly typical, since they are to a large extent conditioned by her character. The only set framework remains the life of Jesus, which constitutes the canon for all ways of perfection. There is no end to the ways his life can be imitated. But the following three truths apply to all: that sacrifice and obedience (as form of love) remain the beginning and the end of mystical experience; that there is no other "dark night" than that of Golgotha (this the sole genuine negative theology); and that there is no internal ascent except the one that becomes realized in Christ's descent. Everything else is left up to God's judgment, and he does not keep to any prescribed gradation but can skip all intervening steps and transport a soul to the highest light and the most perfect purity, then only to plunge it again—for temporal purification or atonement—into all the hells of impurity. Indeed, he can even make a soul stand simultaneously on different steps, since a soul is a wide land: the peaks of the mountains can be radiant with the brightest sunlight while the valleys are covered with fog and rain.

"We can incorporate all ways into our way. In the One Way we include all good ways and not only the specific things of the One. For man must at each moment do only One thing: he cannot do everything. He must at each moment do only One thing; but within this One we ought to encompass all things. God cannot neglect anything, and neither can we neglect anything with God. Therefore, take One Thing from God and draw all that is good into it."

MEISTER ECKHART

People find fault with the Catholic's feeling of superiority. But how could the fact that he has been put right in the center of truth (even if through pure grace) not have an effect, too, on his feelings about life? To be able to judge the parts (the sects, the sector) from the perspective of the whole; to see without being seen; to weigh without being weighed, in the sense of Paul's affirmation: "The spiritual man judges all things but is himself judged by no one." Catholic writers have often tried to imitate the anguished "existentialist" tone of their Protestant counterparts, but that garment does not fit them any better than his father's top hat fit Little Johnny Upstart.

There exists an analogy for man's cooperation in the work of redemption. The lowest step, which is the minimum activity, is the wholly passive condition of allowing oneself to be redeemed, and this is what the Protestant Reformers made to be the norm.

It can be an act of self-humbling for me to be the way to God for another person, with my whole humanity. This can go so far that I am not allowed to disappear in order to show God but must show myself in order to be for that other person an occasion for him to see God in me.

Une âme doit être d'autant plus active qu'elle est plus contemplative: "The more contemplative a soul is, the more active it ought to be."   CONSUMMATA

Souls who love are apostolic already by virtue of their sheer love. It is not as if God owed these souls other souls out of justice; it is just that all love as such is fruitful and redeems.

At Christ's birth Mary was the symbol of the holy vessel that merely contains; and yet she did nourish the Child with her own milk.

The Evangelists show how much God used men's natural characters in order to reveal specifically divine attributes. The typically Lucan theme of the saint as a passive vessel of grace, for instance, is much more than just a typically Lucan theme: it is already a living revelation of a specific trait of Christ and of God himself. The same could be said, not only for all other hagiographers, but for each human being and every creature whatsoever.

Contemplation not before and after but within action. This is meant ontologically and not temporally, for it goes without saying that we have to have regularly appointed times of prayer. Judging by the temporal dimension, there are different types of piety: we can compare Catherine of Siena, for instance, who out of long and solitary periods of prayer "erupts" into sudden action, with Little Thérèse, who acts only in contemplation, or with Saint Ignatius, who contemplates in action! But, ontologically speaking, the same law holds for all precisely because, in contrast to Buddhism and Platonism, it is the law of Christ. All of his activity is a liturgical service before the Father, and, thus, all of his activity is prayer, and all of his prayer is an action and a sacrifice for men before God. All of his prayer leads of itself to action, and all of his activity becomes a prayerful glorification of the Father because of its generosity and its sacrificial character.

The relationship between the apostle's activity and God's activity through him is analogous to the relationship between the physical and the spiritual strengthening that occurs in Holy Communion.

All good and great things automatically build around

themselves a protective layer. It lies in their nature to be esoteric. It is good that this is so, and we should resist the temptation to thwart this principle by making the private public, regardless of how urgent the need may appear.

The heresiarch has followers, the philosopher has disciples, but the apostle has nowhere to lay his head.

Spiritual direction. One should neither lay down one's burden, seeking too easy a relief, nor believe that the conversation follows a psychological and psychoanalytical pattern. The direction of human beings by human beings is quite simply a consequence of the law of Christ's Incarnation and of the structure of his Church. Here, too, humility and obedience are the core principles. The (inevitable) personal element, too, must be a function of the director's objective, ecclesial role, even in the most intimate friendship.

Priest and artist meet along their way. Ridiculed by the crowd, ignored by most, the artist walks ever more decidedly beyond the bounds of the familiar, and, along with him, his art outgrows conventionality and penetrates the sphere of the unique, to the very limit of self-expression: we think of Michelangelo, Mozart, Hölderlin, Schubert. In glacier solitudes the artist falls prey to God. The priest, on the contrary, takes his departure from God and walks ever more deeply into the world. He distributes himself like bread and, in the end, becomes like Orpheus, torn by the maenads limb from limb. Self-outpouring is the essence of both priest and artist: this is their only concern, this their common fate.

In two places in creation the string of the bow spanning matter and spirit is almost violently overstrung. In the natural realm, this occurs in the place of the sexual and in its ambiguity (symbolized by the double function of the reproductive and excretive organs). In the supernatural realm, it occurs in the place of the Church and her essential, irreducible ambiguity, which consists of the poles of authority and obedience, exposed sinfulness and exemplary holiness.

Marriage and celibacy are the two states of life in the Church. We should not make these categories fuzzy and attempt to set up a third possibility between them, such as the idea of a "cloister in the world". Rather, we should try to reflect something of virginity within marriage: that is, virginity as the quality of being free for God within the network of human ties. Reciprocally, we should also seek to reflect something of marriage within celibacy: in the midst of our being free for God, far from taking a thievish pleasure in the thought that we have been spared the "cross of marriage", we should not try to shake from our shoulders the salutary, if heavy, yoke of human bonds and fidelity.

It is not difficult to produce an interesting religious phenomenon at the borderline between Catholicism and heresy. Here a connection between profundity and demonism occurs all by itself (as in the cases of Pascal, Baudelaire, Strindberg, Kierkegaard, Dostoyevsky, and Bloy, among others). To renounce the demonic and develop the fullness of the subjective from the bright center of the Church—*that* would be the thing!

In reciprocal relations between Protestants and Catholics, the most striking thing is that the latter ignore the former completely and no longer give them a thought: they perceive the Protestant principle as a minus of themselves, something they have clearly penetrated once and for all and have found to be too light, something that basically is not worth the trouble. By contrast, the Catholic is for Protestants an annoyance, a constant object of curiosity: they feel in him the presence of a plus that irritates them, something that they cannot get at and that consequently is always challenging them to produce a contradiction.

Only the person who follows the Church has a sure guarantee that, in his obedience to Christ, he is indeed doing more than following his own higher ideas.

The three stages of Church-mindedness: naïve, critical, assenting. In the third stage one is using one's intellect, more than the mere critic does, who takes scandal at everything ecclesial and must spiritualize everything in order to be able to put up with it. Indeed, one must commit oneself to the Church precisely on account of the scandal. The Church is God's perfect instrument: she deserves our greatest love and our absolute obedience and, at the same time, is most highly qualified to humble us and break our craze for perfection.

A norm for living: What is appropriate for a person whom God has taken as an object?

The past is nothing less than a *fait accompli*: it remains the living root of our future. Whatever it may contain, its rising saps can always be used further and channeled to a good or an evil end: as stimulus, springboard, and challenge, or as habit and paralysis. The past is raw material not only for grace but equally for our freedom, and it always remains open to our freedom's grasp.

Isangelos: "equal to the angels"—a magic word for the early Christians. They envied the angels their ability to live continually in the light of full consciousness and not let a single drop of grace go to waste.

The earthly man already lives in eternity. The true state of affairs is not that this fleeting, temporal existence with all its decisions is a pure here-and-now, followed by the reward or punishment of an eternal beyond as a second existence. Rather, the two are one; one is the reverse side of the other: time is concealed eternity, and eternity is revealed time. The transfigured, paradisaical world is none other than the one in which we presently live, only contemplated with different eyes. The Buddhists and the Alexandrians had many an insight into this matter. And Rilke is right: *Lebendige machen alle den Fehler, daß sie zu stark unterscheiden. Engel (sagt man) wüßten oft nicht, ob sie unter Lebenden gehn oder Toten*: "All of the living commit the error of distinguishing too sharply. Angels, they say, often do not know whether they wander among the living or the dead." During the forty days in which the Risen Lord visibly walked the earth, this very earth was paradise for him, so much so that the disciples could perceive the fragrance of the blessed garden through their own earthly dullness, and they could even make us smell that fragrance through the Resurrection narratives.

What is in us is greater than we are; thus, the content is greater than the vessel. Whether the vessel cracks in the enterprise or merely overflows is a matter of indifference. Only one thing matters: the tidings we bear must go forward.

INDEX OF WRITERS QUOTED